"Life is a journey of self-realization." With its blend of Eastern mysticism and Western culture, Jaz's work is an explosive expression of her spiritual journey through the stages love, liberation and self-realization externalized in her art and writings

Jaz writes with compassion, honesty, and warmth, by creating a new path toward spiritual growth and soul renewal. Every piece of her writings and art works reflects her spirit and soul in the most sincere way. ***Journey of The Soul*** will inspire you to discover our purpose in this world, our connections with others, and the beauty of our life through self realization, even though the individual soul is solitary.

All art works in this book created and copyrighted by Jaz Xu
Some pieces of writing translated from the Chinese
by Bruno Alabiso in collaboration with the Author

Copyright © 2019 by Jaz Xu (Jaz 简之)
All rights reserved.
ISBN: 9781712215692

Published and Printed in the United States of America

FOR THE ONES I LOVE

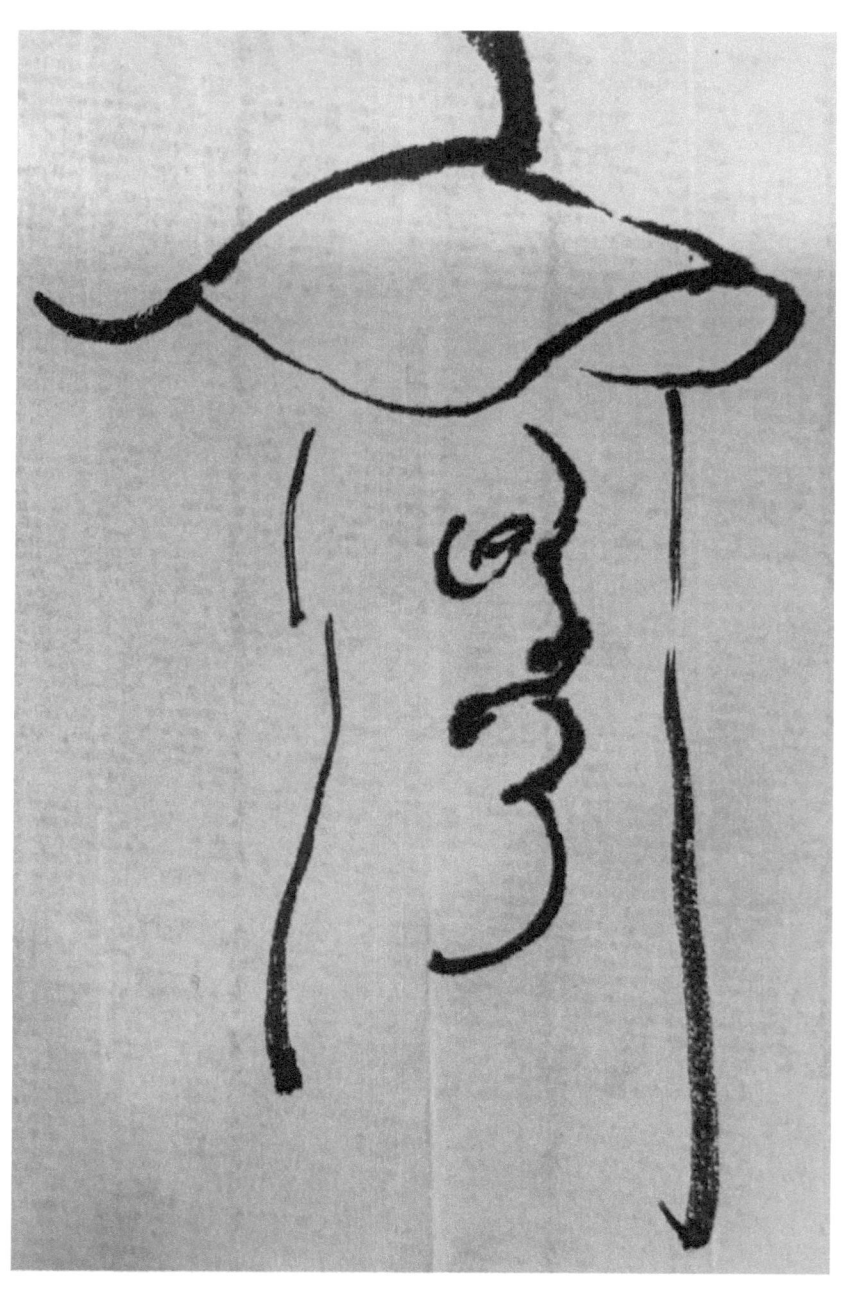

Self Portrait, Ink, by Jaz Xu

Journey of The Soul

Life Journey of Self Realization Through Word And Art

By

JAZ XU

Table of Contents

Introduction	2
Walking Into Middle Ages	5
A Special Kind of Love	17
Soul Mates	22
Our Incompatible Views	27
Forgive and Forget	35
The Purpose of Life	38
First Love	44
Where's My Home	48
My Love Is Not In Madrid	53

Blowing Wind	**61**
A Short Story	**66**
Jacaranda	**70**
The Diamond Life	**77**
My Art Journey	**82**
Promise	**86**
Loving Yourself	**92**
A Story of Past	**100**

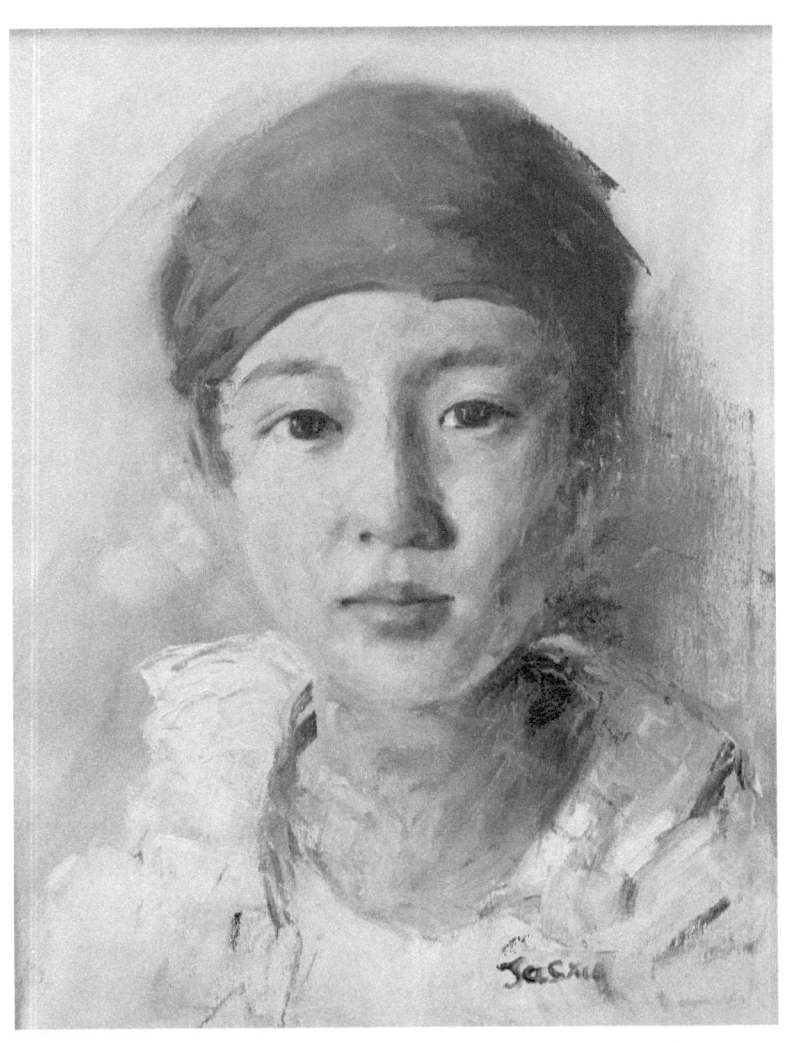

Audrey, Oil, by Jaz Xu

Introduction

I met Jaz a few years ago. We had both been invited by a common friend to a restaurant in Seattle's Chinatown. On that occasion, we did not speak much to each other. And yet, at that very time, I knew instinctively that this woman lived in a deep and rich inner world. Her thick black hair, draped like a privacy curtain in front of her face, could not completely hide the powerful, fiery, mysterious, wild spiritual powers that hid behind it.

After that time, a long time passed before, out of sheer serendipity, we started meeting again. As I enjoyed the long chats we had, where I was mostly a listener and she was the talker. I was blessed to discover the intricate, complex, magnificent presence of her spirit. The more I got to know her, the more I realized that every element of her outer world (the deliciously ambiguous art pieces, the captivating prose and the mystical poetry in particular) was a manifestation of an unusually pure soul.

As our meetings became more frequent, her stories and thoughts assembled magically into a dreamlike mosaic of incomparable beauty, through which I could start to appreciate the significance of her deepest self. Her hair started to part, her eyes sparkled like two diamonds and her smile filled the whole universe.

    Jaz is a very unusual being. Fragile and strong at the same time, she opened her soul for me to discover that my own soul perfectly reflected in hers. I believe that this is her spiritual power: to show others how to find, by means of mirror-like reflection, the forgotten essence of their own soul. So let yourself be touched by the bewitching effect of Jaz' soul.

    Every page in this book gives the reader an opportunity to be caressed by Jaz' crystalline spirit, which she delivers as a gift to everybody who wishes to receive it. Relax all your expectations: Jaz is no ordinary lady, and she knows it well. She is the ultimate solitary traveler, across physical and metaphysical spaces. Traveling with her is bound to give you an opportunity to grow out of the confines of the conventional world and to sprout wings of your own.

(by Bruno Alabiso)

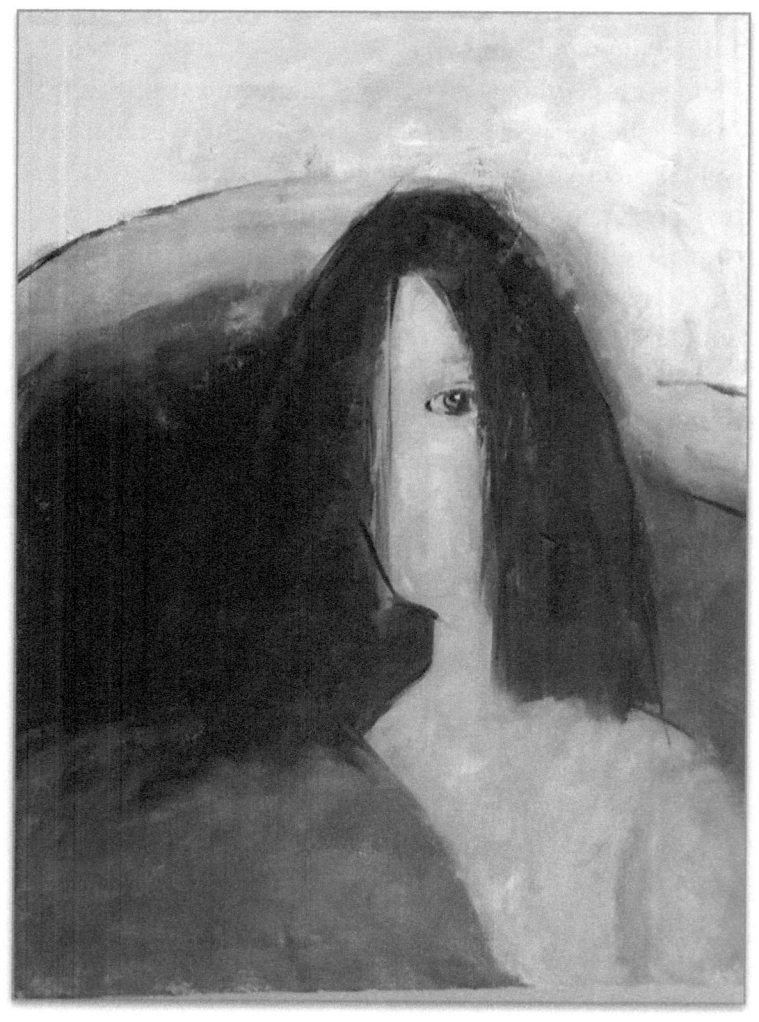

Self Portrait, Oil, by Jaz Xu

Walking Into Middle Ages

Morning has broken. Madrid was sleeping, and I was walking.

As time went by, the sun gradually rose up, and the ground started to warm up. Hot air from the warmed ground was continually warming the soles of my shoes and spreading around. The policemen at the Atocha train station were fully armed, as they were patrolling the place. I fixed my gaze on them for a moment. I was thinking to take a photo with them. They looked at me and smiled with a serious frown. I dismissed the idea of taking a group photo with them, but instead, as I was approaching quite close, I picked up my phone and stole a few shots.

Atocha train station was the largest railway station in Madrid. Its architecture was simple, unadorned. The station was fully functional, uncluttered by the dazzling spectacle of complex luminous neon lights flashing to capture the traveler's attention. Instead, there was a large area of lush vegetation indoors, as well as an elegant coffee shop immersed in the green and some lifelike sculpted suitcases. The passengers sat around the sculptures. Seen from afar, they too looked like they were part of the sculptures.

The train station had three floors, each with a group of platforms. A passenger going to a destination needed to board a station near the corresponding platform. I proceeded to a platform on the second floor, where I would board a train heading to Toledo, an ancient medieval city which was the capital of the Kingdom of Spain from the 6th to 16th century AD.

While still in Madrid, a lady from Portugal had reminded us that, if there were enough time, we should visit Toledo. As a matter of fact, Toledo was a place I didn't want to miss during my trip to Spain. Once there, I would explore the essence of Spanish history, architecture, culture, art, and so on. Toledo was also like a time tunnel which would allow me to travel back to the Middle Ages.

The train was slowly entering the Toledo station under the warmth of the summer sun, already quite high in the sky. From the train station, there were quite a few buses which transported people to the ancient city. However, I didn't want to miss the opportunity to admire the city as it slowly showed up in the distance, so I chose to walk under the scorching sun.

Far in the distance, the entire ancient city of Toledo gradually appeared in front of me, sitting on the hillside, surrounded by ancient walls. The Tagus River at the feet of the ancient city wall flowed peacefully. It looked like the moat that surrounded most of the ancient cities. Perhaps the choice to build this city was based on the observation that this natural moat would make it an ideal military defense feature, at a time when firearms were still absent. Toledo became a battleground for the rulers of various ethnic groups which were trying to dominate Spain.

    I walked on the southern bank of the river and looked at the ancient capital built on the northern bank. As I got closer to the St. Martin Bridge, which connected the opposite banks, ancient buildings appeared gradually, stacked from the bottom of the mountain all the way to the top. As I reached the observation point on the other side of the river, I decided to stop for a moment, and looked at the magnificent arches under the St. Martin Bridge. The river has flowed through the arches for thousands of years. I shifted my gaze back from the bridge to this ancient capital city. What kind of mystery was there waiting for me? I knew the city itself was a big treasure, a giant museum. Centuries came and went, governments changed, history advanced at a steady pace, but this medieval city, which had experienced thousands of years of vicissitudes, still revealed itself to me in its intact form, gleaming in its beauty, and waiting for me to explore, experience, discover, and feel.

    As soon as I stepped onto the "Puente de San Martin" and passed the gate of the Gothic-style defense tower on the bridge, I sensed that I had entered the Middle Ages.

At the entrance to the gate below the bridge tower, I looked at the carvings of each place and marveled at the highly developed craft of that era. At the same time, I touched the old iron veneer that covered the gate of the bridge tower. The patchwork of iron nails inserted in the veneer looked like fragments of history describing the hardship of past lives. Looking back at the bridge, I imagine the architect Juan Guas leading the craftsmen around the clock. Was the arch under the bridge going to be able to withstand the weight of thousands of horses passing through? It was said that he made a mistake in the design: the arches were built in the typical gothic style, with a pointy apex at the top, aesthetics being his main concern. His design neglected to take into consideration the bearing capacity of the structure. What would happen if the bridge collapsed? Although I couldn't confirm whether the following story was true or not, I chose to believe it. On a night swept by high winds, the architect's smart and courageous wife built a fire under the arch. Since the cement between the stones was not completely solidified, the pointed arch collapsed. The architect was then able to rebuild the arch in the present shape, this time redesigned to withstand heavy loads. Not only was the bridge preserved and its strength improved, but the husband's reputation was also saved. We find women with similar abilities and political integrity both in Western and Eastern history.

On the two sides of the bridge, right at the middle point, lied the observation decks, shaped like round brackets. The observation decks allowed monitoring the surroundings on either side of the bridge. From there, one could see hills, mountains, rivers, fields, all contributing to a magnificent view. At the end of the day, I had the opportunity to see the scenery at sunset, and the experience was totally different.

I stood on the observation deck and stroked the stone ball on the top of one of the bridge pillars. I leaned against the railing and faced the bridge. I was not looking at the scenery. Instead, I was looking at a beautiful medieval princess. She was looking back at the castle which stored many memories of her. She was also looking at her heart broken mother. Her charming eyes were filled with tears. She knew it was a final goodbye, a journey without return. She knew she would never have a chance to return to her homeland, but she might not have known that this was also a life-ending journey. Did her father, the first Visigoth king who built the capital in this ancient city, feel his heart filling with compassion? Was there any grief in his heart? Or was the daughter just an object of transaction, a victim of political trading?

The beautiful princess reluctantly continued to walk along the bridge. Her horse was laden with the dowry. The animal seemed to know the master's mind and slowly walked forward. The princess passed by my side, and when she reached the front of the tower, she stopped. She once again turned back her head. Her eyes were full of sadness, resentment and disappointment, but they were also filled with trepidation. What was she looking forward to? What about her beloved knight? Where was he? Was he still looking at his beloved woman who had slipped away from him, while he was standing among the crowd? The pain was intense, a kind of pain she had never experienced before. Perhaps the only thing the knight could do was to silently wish her happiness. What he certainly did not expect was that his beloved princess not only would fail to reach happiness, but later die of a violent death by the hands of her husband. I averted my gaze from the sight of the princess' beautiful and sad eyes, because my own eyes were also full of tears.

I left the bridge and passed through the last magnificent bridge tower. I looked at the double eagle badge on a pylon. It was a very domineering city emblem. Every detail was full of history, culture and art.

Once climbing at the top of the stairs made of stone, I officially entered the ancient city. Was I there to help the Princess realizing the dream of returning homeland? Perhaps I was longing for my own hometown.

In the summer afternoon, the sun was getting hotter, the backpack on my back was getting heavier, and tiny rivulets of sweat ran down my back. However, there was no discomfort in the shade of the olive trees. The breeze blew through and it was very refreshing. The Toledo's climate is similar to that of the West Coast of the United States. It is a hot and dry climate. I sat down to rest. There weren't many pedestrians around. The birds were hovering in the air, they seemed to outnumber the people on the ground. Toledo was a very quiet ancient city。

The hotel was near the center of the city. Many steps made of stone leaded to a cobblestone path. At the end of the path was the door of the hotel. There were two Chinese couples in the hotel's courtyard. They were taking pictures of each other. They asked me to take their photo.

People from the same homeland act more cordially when they meet abroad.

    The hotel was a small guest house, itself a medieval building, and of course it was also the private residence of a white-haired old lady. Through the window of the room, I could see all kinds of ancient buildings in the distance. I put down my backpack, and the sun in the yard under the window was just right. I was preparing to go out, when a woman suddenly showed up in front of me in the living room and scared the life out of me. Was this a real person? Or was she a princess who travelled from the Middle Ages? From her appearance she didn't look like a princess. She looked more like a deformed wandering woman. Two empty big eyes were inlaid in her small face. Maybe she had some genetic defects which caused her figure to become deformed. She came to greet me. I got a little scared, even though it would have been easy for me to push her away, since she was so light and small. She didn't look like an average looking woman. Her figure looked like an undernourished person from Africa. However, she seemed fleshier, less bony than a person suffering from undernourishment. I looked around, there was no one. She was speaking to me, and she was speaking in Spanish. I told her in English that I didn't speak her language. She took out her phone and used a 'speaking' translator to allow me to understand what she was saying. I also took out my mobile phone and translated what I wanted to say into Spanish. This way, we could communicate with each other.

    She told me she was a homeless, a 19 years old girl. She had been driven out of her house by her family (in this aspect, her story was similar to the princess's). She lived in the street with her boyfriend. The local church had given her some money, so she was able to stay at the hotel for one night. The money was not enough for two people, so her boyfriend had to sleep outside that night. I looked at her: what kind of man would want such a woman to be his girlfriend? She seemed to anticipate my question, and she showed me a photo on her phone. Her boyfriend was a handsome, healthy man. She had been driven out of the house because she had fallen in love with him. The man also loved her, so he decided to stay with her against the objections of his family. For various reasons, at that time there was scarcity of employment in Spain. Many people could only live in the streets. But the couple loved each other very much and they didn't want to be separated (while she was communicating with me, her boyfriend had called several times). What kind of love was this? Of course, it was a love that had not been blessed by the families. I didn't fully understand, I didn't know how to judge. Maybe I didn't need to understand or judge. Perhaps, their love was true love: true love did not have a justification, was not subjected to conditions, couldn't be given up and it did not tolerate separation. Maybe the story of her love and her present emotional state had moved me. Maybe her desolate life on the streets had filled me with compassion. Maybe when she guessed that I must be 23 years old made me happy. In any case, I gave her all the snacks and fruits I had previously bought before coming to the hotel. Generosity also causes the giver to receive something: the good feeling of giving. When you give food to people who need it, a scent remains in your heart, the 'scent of generosity'. That could be satisfying more than eating the food yourself. I left the hotel and my heart couldn't wait to speed walk through this ancient medieval city.

I strolled through the intricate network of cobblestone streets, I didn't want to miss a single alley. The bricks, stones, wood, tiles and mud here seemed to tell their story. Every time I entered a church, a museum or any buildings that piqued my curiosity (I had bought a pass for museums, churches, art galleries, etc.), I started to explore. I climbed the spire of the Toledo Cathedral, once a mosque. The cathedral overlooked the entire city. I visited the quiet Catholic church and glanced at the remains of the pope in the center of the church. I stared at the impressive, simply adorned, quaint city gate, built in Byzantine style: the Puerta del Sol (they say that the Puerta del Sol was on the zero degree meridian and it was exposed to the sun all day long). So much history had passed through these roads. So many works of art, so many architectural styles left their mark on the place. Of course, I also came across a lot of local folklore and specialties as I walked through the narrow streets.

From one street to the other, a spiraling flock of birds crossed the sky above the pedestrians walking in the ancient streets: they were at the same time peaceful and auspicious. The narrow cobblestone streets formed a labyrinth, as they snaked between religious synagogues, royal palaces, museums, monasteries, temples, and so on. There was no modern building there. Toledo was not only the center where three major religions intertwine, but it was also the residence of the Spanish cardinal.

As the sun gradually descended, I walked out of the city to reach the opposite bank of the river. I climbed to the highest point of the hillside, and finally sat down on a stone. I just sat quietly, watching the ancient capital city bathed in the sunset, like a perfect piece of art. I stared for a long time and etched a memory of it deep into my heart.

The sun set and the sky were full of clouds. Before the sun disappeared in the west, I went down the hillside and returned to the bridge. I stepped onto the bridge and watched the last sunset until the first artificial lights of the city illuminated the streets.

I continued to stroll through the winding medieval streets, looking back and forth at buildings of different styles, Gothic, Moorish, neo-classical, Baroque etc. Time seemed to have turned back, back to the era of Cervantes, the knights, the castles, the ancient churches. Knives and swords, love and hate. The blessing of time and the mercy of the elements had transformed all into a solemn hall, an ancient wall, smooth pebbles, silent sculptures, melodious bells, and the sounds of birds singing in the sky.

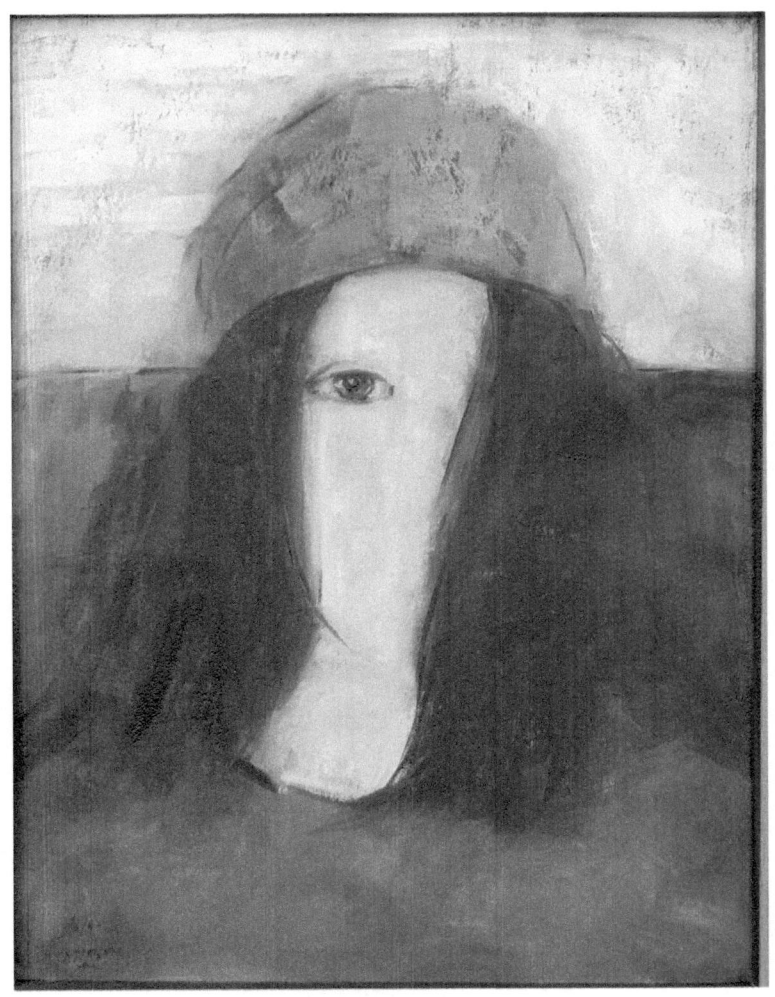

Self Portrait, Oil, by Jaz Xu

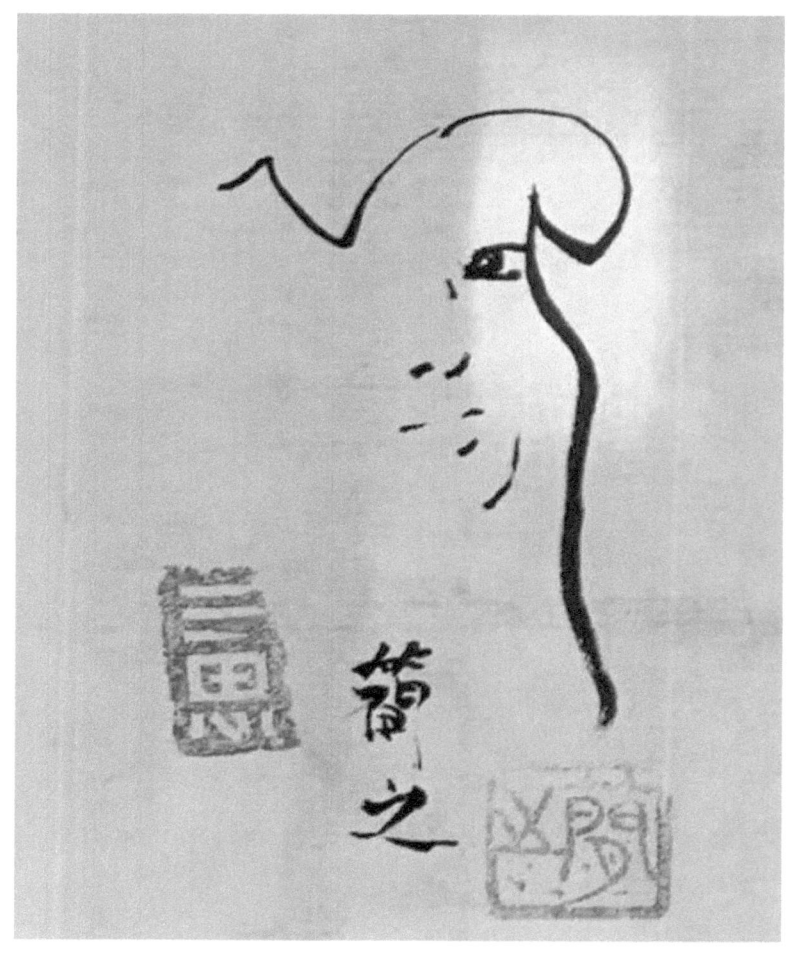

Self Portrait, Ink, by Jaz Xu

A Special Kind of Love

IT was Valentine's Day, a romantic day. Almost all the ladies were expecting flowers from their loved ones.

It was also a special day, sunny and breezy, worth remembering. Mother and I were talking about my younger self, the one who was energetic, free-spirited, daring, unconventional, the one who crossed the pacific ocean all the way from the little island on the east to the big land of the west, and the one who never acted in an ordinary way, who could cross over dead bodies without any fear, calm and still, or even brave enough to walk across the graves alone before dawn.

I don't know when that peculiar young version of me started to gradually disappear, to be replaced by a shadow of myself. It seemed like I was living for the responsibility of taking care of others. There was no thought for myself, my own needs. My role was that of a housewife. Children and chores were the only things that kept me occupied. I metamorphosed into a traditional housewife doing busy housework while taking care of my growing kids. Nevertheless, in the few periods of free time which were left in my busy daily schedule, I occasionally gave myself the opportunity to enjoy art, music and other pleasures of life.

However, there was an alternative way I could have chosen to live, a way that would have allowed me to follow my inner voice, to be a woman who would have been happy no matter whom she would marry, no matter what situations she would encounter, as the source of the joy would not be to rely on her life companion or the things she engaged into, but would be a manifestation of the spirit that resided deeply inside of her.

I hoped I would be a woman who whether was loved or not, she would be fine, and whether was cared for or not, she would be calm and peaceful, and she could always be calm and peaceful no matter what happened to her. However, I, fortunately or not, do love in a deep way. Because of the deep love, I experiences joy as well as pain; because of what I experienced, I grew; and because of the growth, I learnt more about the essence of love. The best love is to make oneself become authentic through the experiences of life and love.

Who am I? This question had been always in my mind since I was still a little child. I found the answer a long time ago. How could I become the authentic version of myself? It seems that the real 'me' appeared, disappeared, reappeared, and disappeared again. At the end, that 'me', my true nature clearly revealed.

"Don't forget your original heart, and go find your real self.", a deep inner voice has always been reminding me. To find my real self is not just my wish but it is also the practical way to develop an authentic personality.

I looked back and reviewed my experiences in the past, no matter whether they were good or bad: they had all been drowned in the torrent of time, just like the tears disappear in the rain. There was nothing to complain or regret about.

"Life is a journey, and the most important time is 'now', the present moment I'm in", I said to myself. I felt my true self, was back. Maybe it had never been lost, it had only been neglected. At that moment, I felt I was like a butterfly coming out of the cocoon, spreading its wings and starting to fly.

On this special day, with the deep love I felt for myself, I wanted to say to this authentic me:

"A special kind of love to you".

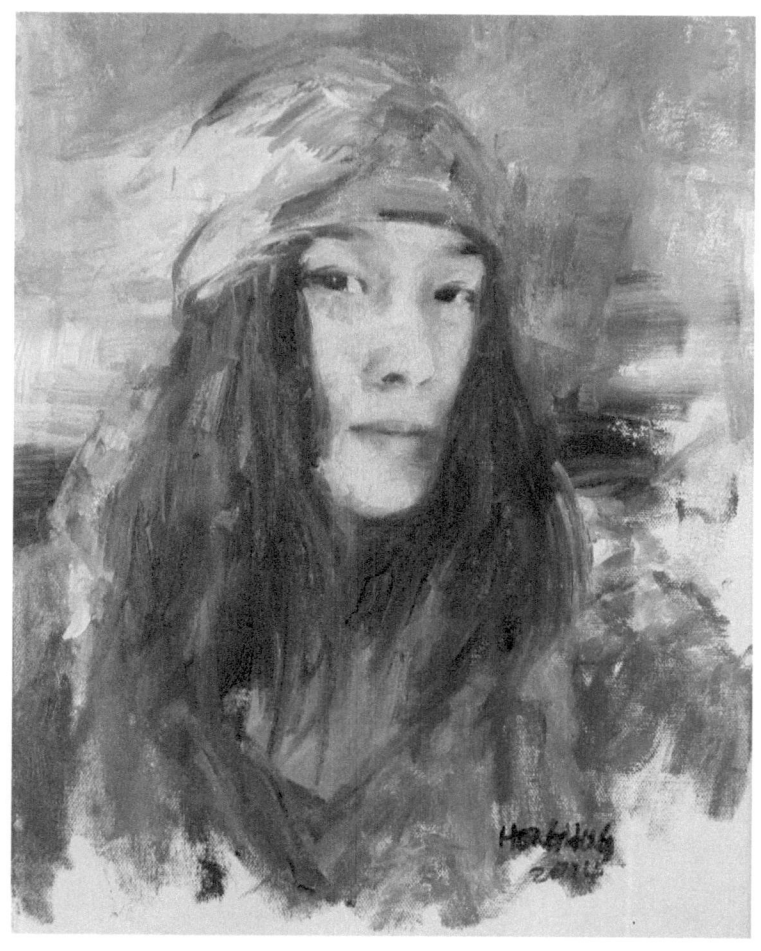

Self Portrait, Oil, by Jaz Xu

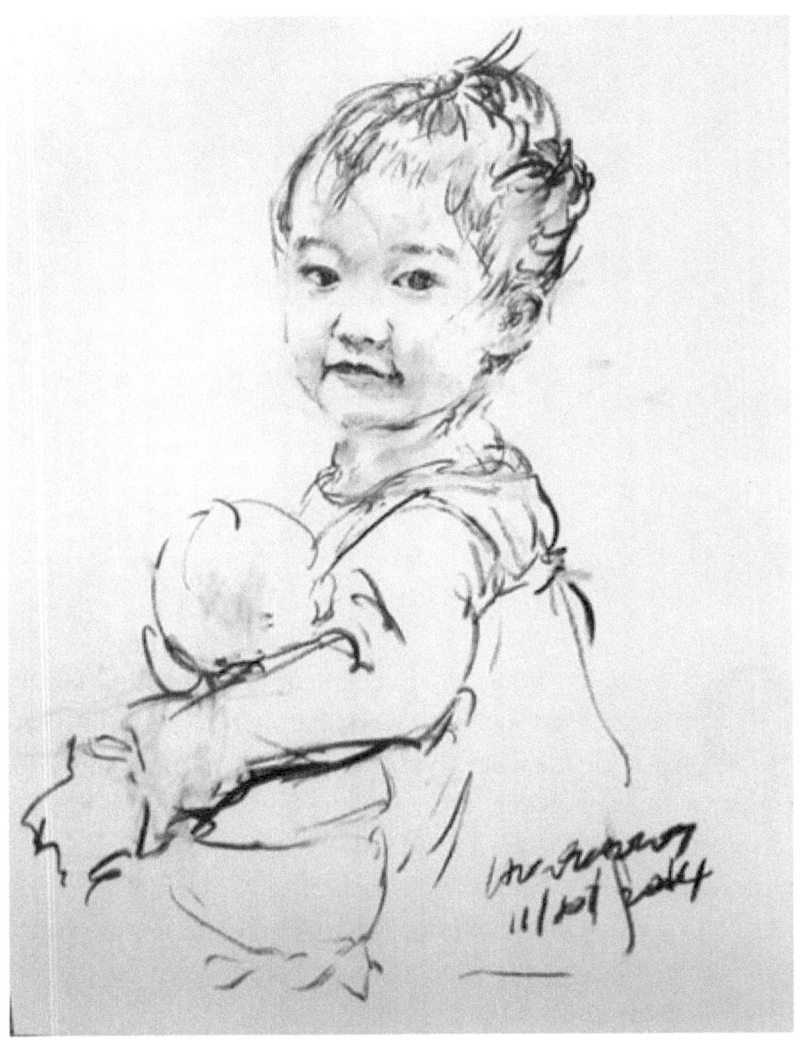

Abby, Oil, by Jaz Xu

Soul Mates

Outside the window, two splendid butterflies are playing among the flowers, bathing in the light of the sun. They are flying up and down, incessantly playing with each other, and skirting the blooming field. I've been staring at them for a while. What nourishes them the most is not the ocean of flowers, but each other.

As we live in this world, our true nourishment is not fame and wealth, but the spontaneous love between people, as well as the nobility of our souls.

As the world becomes more and more diversified, complicated, attractive, our materialistic desires are awakened, and we become mesmerized by the multitude of colors therein. However, our hearts feel more and more empty and lonely, as the souls seem to drift away in anguish. In this hustle and bustle world, our hearts are impetuous. It's hard to maintain the nobility of our souls while drifting in the whirlwind of despair. It's also difficult to find a pure love while in the throngs of earthly sensuality.

If the nature of soul is truly noble, then the deepest and truest love between people should be the deepest connection between the souls, the recognition of the mutual dependence of the souls, the mutual awakening and comforting of the souls and hearts. Because the souls connect to each other, love can last forever, as its spirit stretches to infinity. And this love begins and ends with the soul's connection.

The true partner is your 'soul mate'. But what do we mean by 'soul mate'?

A soul mate is a person who explores the mystery of life with you. He or she is somebody who unconditionally appreciates you for who you are. Somebody who has reunited with you countless times in the deepest corners of the world. Somebody who gives your life a sense of accomplishment and allows you to enter higher and deeper levels of existence.

When you meet a soul mate, your heart awakens fully in the most authentic way. That match is perfect.

True love is the love expressed by the heart and the soul.

The love between souls manifests when two souls are mysteriously looking at each other in hearts. This love bridges the chasm that separates two hearts. The result is a profound appreciation and a full comprehension of love itself. This love cherishes and preserves the absence of desire. It focuses on a deep concern for the present moment.

However, not everyone seeks to live in the heart and soul. It's impossible for a person who cannot perceive his own soul to experience soul-level love. A person who does not know how to give love can hardly meet his or her soul's intimate friend.

If a person's soul never meets a kindred spirit, it becomes a lonely soul drifting away in the darkness of the night. There is no one to connect with and there is no direction to follow. Lonely and empty fragments of time fill the bottom of the heart.

The quality of the experience of receiving and offering love affects the quality, the happiness and the meaning of life itself.

The lack of loved ones produces loneliness. The unloving soul greatly suffer from it. The souls that do not find a good fit with others are lonely. A soulless life is sad.

On the other hand, life with soul-level love is full of spirit, full of energy, unique, as it allows one to live to the extreme, immersed in spiritual pleasure, inner joy and inner wealth.

The love of the spirit is the highest form of love. Recognizing each other at the spirit level is like finally being able to see the world's true beauty. From then on, there isn't any longer a landscape for the eyes to see.

Life is a long journey, and you will visit innumerable places. May you have a soul mate who perfectly fits your spirit and takes your soul by the hand. May your souls 'talk' with each other about romantic love until the end of the world, may they look after each other in this life and meet again in future lives.

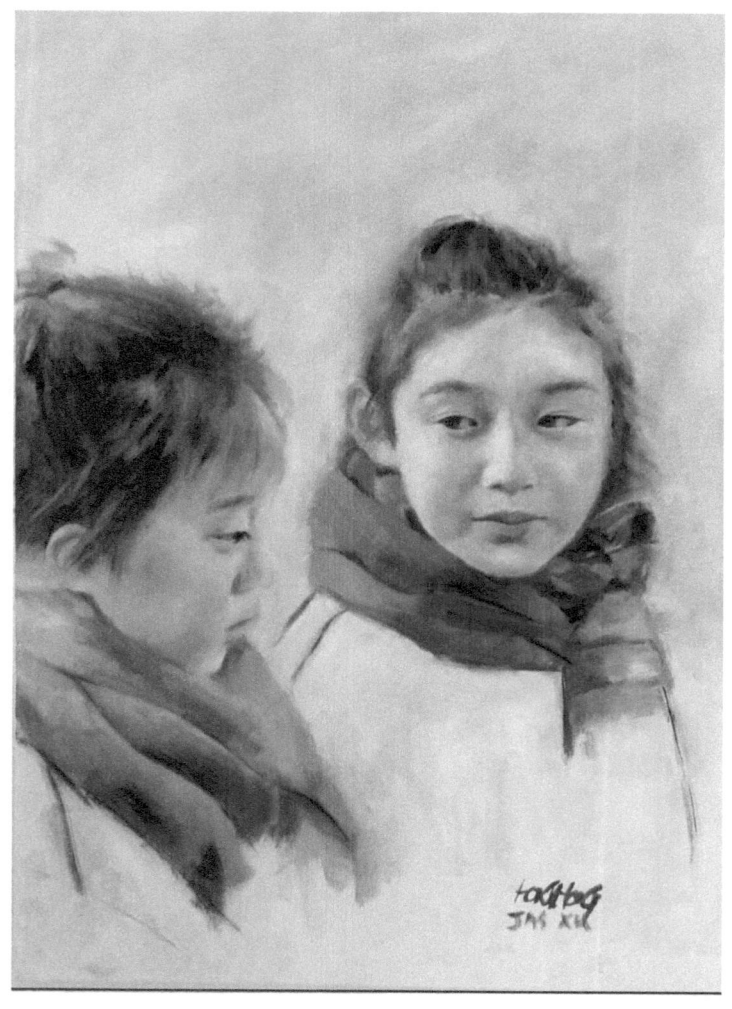

Sisters, Oil, by Jaz Xu

Our Incompatible Views

He said: "We've broken up because our views are incompatible at a fundamental level".

She said: 'We got divorced because our views did not match"

He said: "I've been looking for someone whose ideas resonate with mine. This someone is hard to find. But I so desire that my other half could have the same views as mine".

In fact, I also want to have a true soul mate with the same fundamental views. As I explained in my previous article, soul mates can be discovered, but cannot be sought. I believe that they do exist, but you need to understand what each other's fundamental views are real matching.

I have a good friend who has a similar soul to mine. We have the same views on many things such as life, art, literature, and travel, etc. However, when we dig deeply, we discover we also hold many different views. Luckily, we have the same attitude: we accept and respect our reciprocal views.

Indeed, when we reach a state when we do not understand what the other party says or thinks, as illustrated in the saying: "the three fundamental views do not match", we feel tired of the relationship, as it seems that nothing can be explained clearly. The language itself becomes a source of misunderstanding.

But we have overlooked one simple fact: there are no two completely identical people in the world. Everyone is an independent individual, with a different personality. People are so different in many ways: they come from different families, they have different backgrounds, have different social environments, and even have different innate DNA structures. All these individual traits produce different personalities.

How can we be completely compatible with all these differences?

Disagreements to be found in the "three fundamental views" are normal, but they are not necessarily the source of the contradiction, the so called "three view incongruity". The real source of contradiction is that, when facing the normal phenomenon of inconsistency, one party uses his/her own views to demand, force or even kidnap the other's point of view, to submit the other party into accepting one's own values, and to disallow the other party from being "different".

So, gradually, we feel more and more tired of our interpersonal relationships, because there is always a person who likes to place his/her own views above the other's, and use them to judge and belittle you, or even beat you up.

Yesterday, a good friend of mine told me that she had been 'unfriended' by a former confidante. He often said she was unique and stood out from all his female friends. He even said that he admired her, which I do not doubt. The reason for unfriending her was simple: she did not agree with some of his views. He could not persuade her otherwise, so he immediately removed her from his social network.

In fact, I would say that getting rid of this type of 'friend' is also a relief. Sometimes when a person's thinking becomes dissonant with that of a close associate, a psychological conflict and discomfort will arise. People will choose the path of minimum resistance, which will save the most energy, in order to change their partner's way of thinking, and to force their partner's views to become consistent with theirs, so as to dispel their own tension. Almost everyone has an original motivation to pursue self-preservation, security, superiority, satisfaction, well-being, and so he/she strives to maintain the "stability" of those feelings.

Once there is a cognitive conflict, it's easy to develop self-protection, and in order to maintain the previously mentioned feelings of self-preservation, security, superiority, satisfaction, and happiness, we tend to think that we are right, and the ones with diverging opinions are wrong. Consequently, we are going to find any possible reasons to disprove, deny, convince, and finally change the other's views to maintain 'cognitive consistency'.

Some people will use their own 'three fundamental views' to give others a self-centered and one-sided version of the facts, in order to prove that their ideas are absolutely right.

Some people also like to use 'right' or 'wrong' to measure the values of both parties, and naturally they will place the 'other' on the 'wrong' side. The reasoning goes something like this: "If I think that you are wrong, I have to convince you and you'd better change your view, otherwise you are the enemy, and therefore no longer a friend." This is the negative effect of *cognitive dissonance.*

A truly mature person knows how to deal with these cognitive dissonances, without rashly interfering with the others. A truly mature person also won't argue with others about non-congruent views, but rather he/she will respect the other's right to express their own opinions. When encountering an inconsistency in the "three fundamental views", he/she will acknowledge the cognitive dissonance, and will avoid using their own argumentations to fight for the victory.

To understand others is not easy. How can we know what is in the mind of others, since sometimes we can't even fully understand ourselves? When we encounter a disagreement, what shall we do in order to free ourselves from the feeling of contradiction, misinterpretation and paradoxes? The secret of keeping the disagreement without feeling uncomfortable is captured in the word "respect".

When you show respect for others, you will not try to resolve conflicts by using your own views, but, instead, you will accept the contradictions arising from the different views, and you will let the two perspectives coexist. So, whether the relationship consists of a beautiful friendship, a sweet love, or other kinds of love, to show mutual understanding, tolerance and *respect* is more important than trying to make the opinions unanimous. Do not fight along the line of 'right' or 'wrong' and do not force others to change, but allow others to be different. In love, try to be inclusive, respectful and understanding.

It's easy to debate by using words like 'good', 'bad', 'right' or 'wrong', but it is important to realize that love trumps all other considerations.

People say that if we allow different opinions to coexist, this will eliminate most of the troubles in the world. True.

A friend said to me: "You can take my house, my car or anything else you like, but you can never take away my freedom". Another friend told me that she quarreled with her husband every day because both of them wanted to change the other's way of thinking. Yet another good friend said to me: "I appreciate and accept you completely just the way you are. If one day you change for my sake, then you will no longer be yourself, and the woman that I appreciate will no longer exist."

In order for us to have a good relationship with others and remain in a state of deep love, it is best to respect each other's unique character and opinions.

I'm thinking about a social media place called 'Moments' where some people post their personal activities, photos, and fun experiences, while some others advertise stuff. For me, that is a place where I can keep my daily memories, my snapshots of life. But it does not matter for what type of reason people post in 'Moments', I do enjoy looking at those snippets, as they provide me with an opportunity to learn about different cultures, share travel experiences, or even get to know good restaurants they recommend .

I believe we are certainly not expecting everyone to live the same life, to say or think the same things. If we all had the same standards for what we like and hate, if we all did the same things and had the same skills, then the world would become a very boring place.

It is indeed the richness of the world that makes us see and enjoy the infinite variety of possibilities opened to us. The abundance of inconsistent and incompatible views provide us abundant life experiences, it allows us to observe the multiplicity of views, hear different stories, and experience the whole extent of human life.

To make our relationships harmonious, we need to seek common ground without necessarily giving up our personal views. We also need to accommodate any "inconsistencies" with the views of others.

As an example, I believe that many readers will hold different views on this article, and I respect their opinions. However, I also want to stress a very important point which is at the base of a balanced relationship with others: in order for us to have the same views, we should have the same vision and the same revelation arise from our deepest spirit, a vision based on love. If we have the same perspectives in our deepest spirit, we could say that our views are congruent, as they spread out from our deepest inside to our souls and bodies.

Journey of The Soul | Jaz Xu

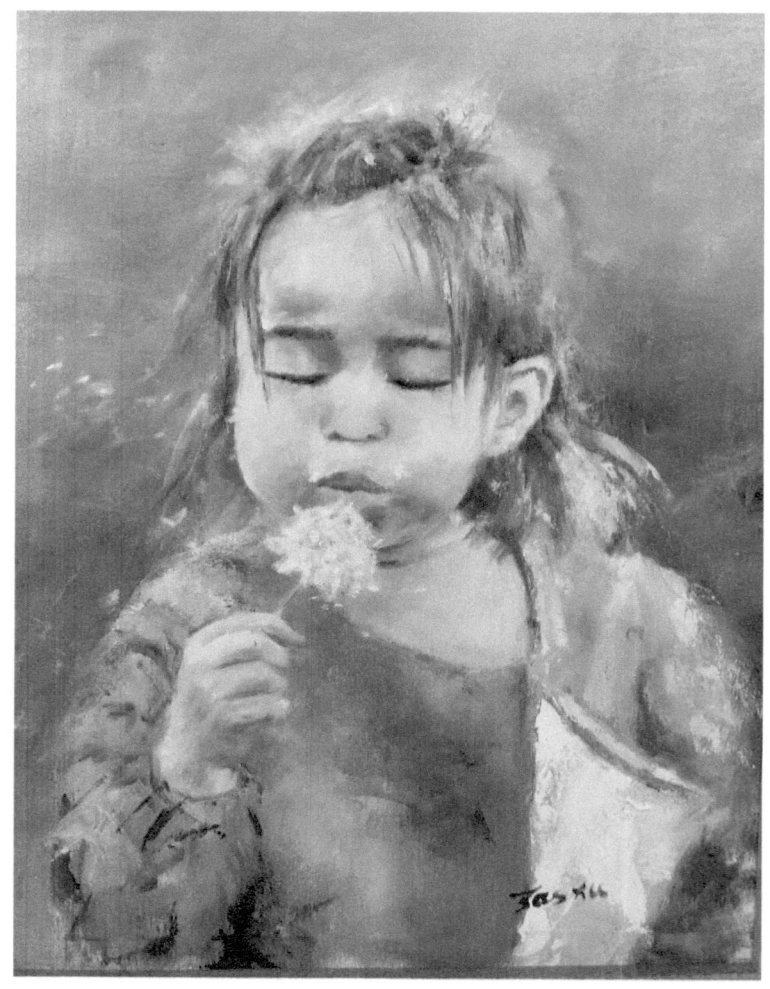

Girl, Oil, by Jaz Xu

Forgive and Forget

I sit quietly, and listen to her grumbling, complaining, and blaming the past while weeping uncontrollably. I don't say anything. I know that being quiet is the best reaction at this moment.

She keeps on talking and complaining. Finally, she's tired. I stand up with a light smile on my face.

"Please take a rest". I whisper to her.

She looks at me awkwardly and says: "I have no intention to complain but I want to talk to you. If I have said anything that hurt you, I want to apologize".

"It's ok, no damage done "I answer quietly.

A feeling of sympathy arises from my heart. I know I am her only source of comfort at this moment. She loves me.

It takes a whole life for people to grow, but it only takes a second to be old.

She's getting old. Her trepidation of becoming old, and the physical pain caused by the disease work together to make her want to vent and grieve. I used to be easily hurt by her words, but now, it does not affect me, I feel rather indifferent. I care for her in a peaceful way and the awkwardness caused by her emotional reaction dissolves into thin air.

She needs me, but she is afraid to bother me. This creates an inner conflict, because she loves me.

I feel compassion for her, and gradually I start to know her better. I don't insist in claiming what I think to be right, wrong, good or bad any more. What I wish for her is peace and joy. Everything which can make her happy is all good and right.

Love or hatred will disappear when the time goes by. To forgive and to forget is the key to happiness. All the pains accumulated in the life of a person will dissolve in time. No matter what happens to you, the wise response is to give thanks.

Life is a process of forgiveness and letting go, and this is also the deepest way to make us peaceful and joyful.

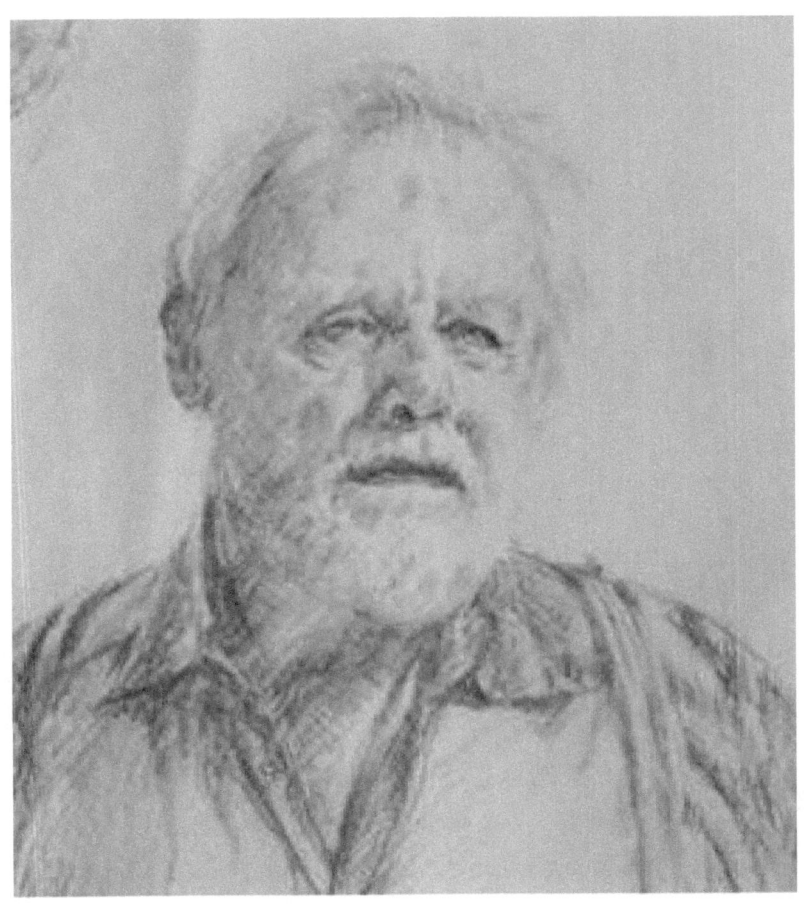

Old Man, Pen, by Jaz Xu

The Purpose of Life

There are always accidents happening at random, and often, out of a sudden, things change. People you know very well may disappear forever, and the places used to be beautiful don't exist anymore. The only thing left behind is grief.

A few years ago a 7.0 earthquake hit a beautiful place in the southwest of China on the night of August 8th. Many houses were torn down and many lives got lost. A beautiful place became a big mess, and many families were heart broken.

There are always some unpleasant events happening in our life. Nothing is more serious than the loss of our own life, and nothing is more painful than the loss of our loved ones. Human beings are so weak, when we encounter an unfortunate accident, we really can't do much.

Beside mourning, have we ever thought about what life is, what the eternity is, and what our life purpose is?

I was lying on a Yoga pad last night, recollecting what I had experienced before. Whether bitter, sweet, sad or joyful, no experience will remain the same with the passage of time, and those original feelings will gradually disappear. I am not a person who particularly enjoys material things, yet this colorful world does occasionally stimulate my desires. When my desires are fulfilled, I am joyful and satisfied for a while. In the long term, I'll never be satisfied by material things. There is neither unceasing joy nor immortal elements in this world.

The human being is the center of this world. God's creation is for Man, and Man's creation is also for Man. However, do we humans feel real satisfaction in those rich and colorful creations?

I continued to recollect my past experiences, and I thought about the gains and the losses. There was never an absolute gain or an absolute loss. No matter how your desires, fame and wealth are fulfilled, no matter how much you immerse yourself in pleasures, no matter how joyful your soul is at any given time, afterwards all the joy is replaced by a feeling of emptiness and solitude deep inside.

Life is the foundation and the essence of human existence in this world. Although many people look at life as a source all kinds of temptations, it is also clear that, without life itself, all human pursuits would be meaningless. We work hard for food, and food is essential to keep us alive. The highest priority need is the need to live. Only when they are physically alive, humans can pursue what makes them happy: riches, fame, fortune, and self-affirmation.

Human life is short, as everything else in this world. Everything will decay and eventually disappear.

When I talk about life, most people think I am talking about the physical life, as I mentioned before. Physical life is short and will end when we stop breathing. However, based on the bible, this type of life is not the real life.

Then, what is the real life? According to the bible, the real life is eternal, it won't disappear. Without this type of life, even if you are physically alive, you are still dead. But with eternal life, even when you are physically dead, you are still alive. This is the eternal life given by the eternal God. God-given life manifests itself in the spirit and in His holy words.

When I was still in college, I acknowledged the spiritual mystery of life, and accepted the holy spirit as my true life and salvation. Each life has its own growth journey and it will gradually be perfected in the process. I'm not the life giver, but the acceptor of this life, the eternal life, and God is the one who makes me grow.

Each man's life has its own limitations. No matter what type of relations we have with others or with ourselves, it's easy for us to be wicked, covetous, malicious, envious, murderous, deceitful, malignant, arrogant, boastful, slandering, faithless, God-hating. At the same time we are also virtuous, helpful, altruistic. Our souls are complicated. It is hard to predict what will go through our minds. We like to judge people and things on the base of our understanding of 'good' or 'bad'.

I love to travel, and I love to be in nature. I used to love to immerse myself in the natural world and to heal the hurt caused by life situations. I felt temporary healed when I faced beautiful and majestic mountains and rivers. However, once I returned back to my daily routine, all the pain reappeared. What really heals us cannot be found in external things, but only in the eternally holy life planted in in us by God.

In those days I often wondered where I would be without God's salvation. Where is my real home, the place where my heart can dwell peacefully? I know that, without Him, my world's desires and pursuits will never be satisfied. What I really want is not the visible material things (even though I may work hard to get some material things for the purpose of physical living). What I need is to go back to the life source.

I was seeking pure everlasting relationships before, but I found out that they do not exist in world of humans.

We've been working hard for our physical life, *but what's the benefit if we win the whole world but lose our soul life?*

I asked God again that night about where my real home is, where my heart's dwelling place is, and what on earth I really wanted.

God said: "I am the true love, the real life, the living water. People who drink the water I give them will never be thirsty again, the life I give them will never end. My love is wide, high, long and deep."

Indeed, if true love and eternal life existed in human beings, then it would not be necessary for God to offer us salvation. Only when we accept the One who is eternal love, light, life, and truth, there will be true love in the world as well as real life in humans.

We pursue so many things in our life, but at the end nothing is more important than life itself and all the love given and received. May we gain the eternal life and everlasting love.

Journey of The Soul | Jaz Xu

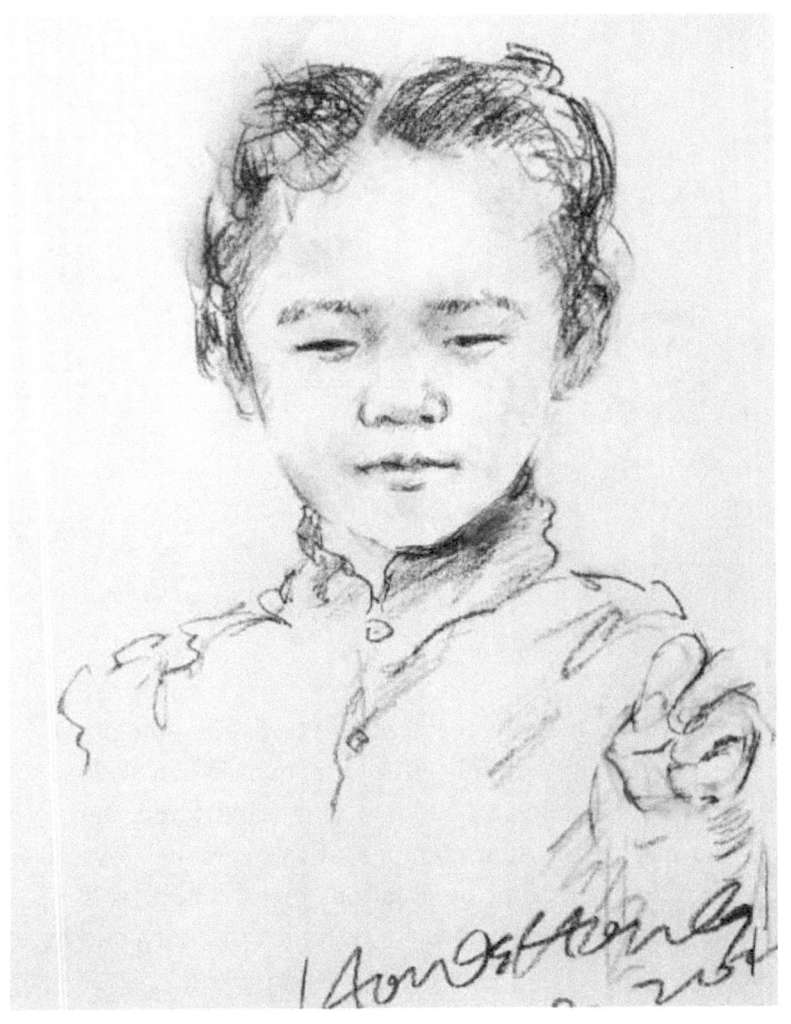

Audrey, Charcoal, by Jaz Xu

First Love

People say that real love makes you blind. It's certainly true for me. When I love someone, I become crazy and blind, and I don't see any of the shortcomings of the person I love. I don't even care what type of situations I may find myself in, and love the one so deep that he becomes the only one in my sight.

People also say he best way to love is to love for love 's sake, to love blindly, without any reason, to love in a way similar to the way I have experienced myself. You can't love properly unless love the one in a blind way, since without that blondness you may see the loved one's shortcomings and decide to leave. That type of love is not pure.

A blind kind of love makes you love the one even he (she) has betrayed you, and that type of love is called the 'first love'. This pure, unconditional and blind love is exactly the type of love that God has for his people.

God loves us unconditionally and blindly, but what about us? We always flee away from this type of first love, and act like homeless people wandering around the world without looking back.

We should let God's love constrain us, we should restore our first love we felt for Him. We should put him first in all situations, and live not only for Him but also live in Him. It's our failure to live without the source of living water - God's presence. It is our failure to abandon our first love.

What we do in our life should be based on our 'first love' for the Lord, since when He returns and we stand before the Judgment bench, He will check on our 'first love' for him. The Lord won't judge us based on what we do for Him but on our capacity to love Him. Our love for the Lord is what makes Him satisfied and joyful. We should give priority to the enjoyment of the Lord, to the love for the Lord, and to the actions caused by our love for Him.

We have the life He gave us, and His life becomes our light. The light shines in darkness, and the darkness never overcomes the light. So, whenever we face darkness, we don't need to remove the darkness but simply come to the light. The darkness will automatically disappear once we come to the light.

Love makes people blind, crazy, and go through many sacrifices. However, God's love is also life and light. We give Him our first love, and His holy spirit, which is also God's love and life, lives within us. With this holy love and life, our lives start to be transformed, and so do our actions. Because we have God's life within us, we can love people through His love, and this love likes the light which is shining in the world.

Journey of The Soul | Jaz Xu

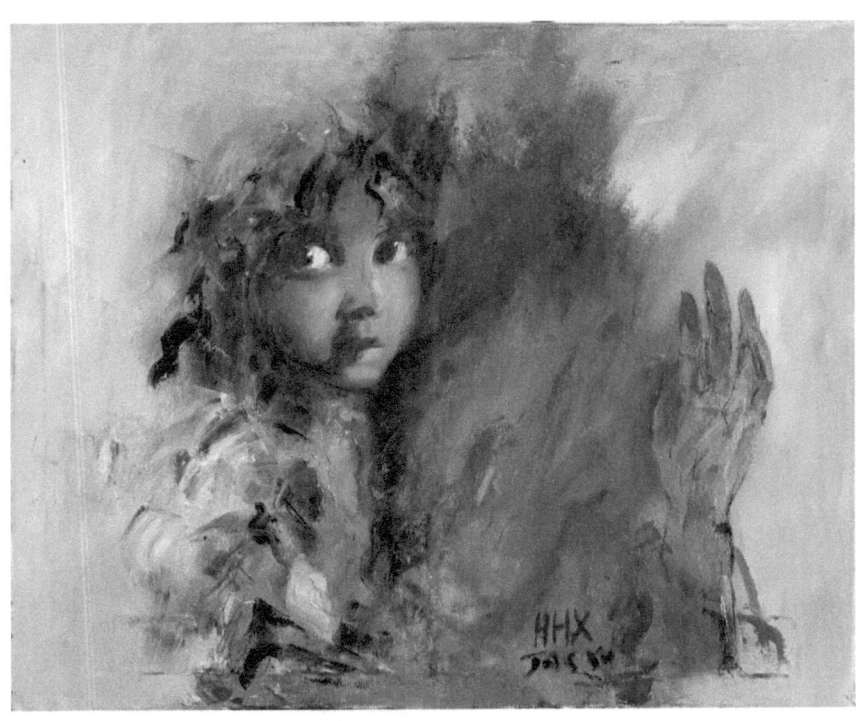

Where is My Home, Oil, by Jaz Xu

Where's My Home

Whether it is the pastoral places in Tao Yuan Ming's poems, or the huts in Du Fu's poems; whether it is the Tian family in "The Village of Times bygone" or the River Continent in the Book of Poems; whether it is nostalgia evoked by a poem, or sorrow evoked by a painting, everyone has a home in their hearts, a place where the body and mind can rest.

From the time we are toddlers, children, adolescents, youth, middle-aged, till the time we are old, some live in the same house and place for the whole life, while others live everywhere around the world. This type of residential space we live in, called house 'home', protects our bodies, shelters us from wind and rain, and in the summer shields us from the heat. It is our place of body rest.

In life there are always people concerned about our safety, people who understand our weakness, rejoice in our joyous moments, accompany us in our sorrow, as we give and receive love. They are our friends, the loved ones, the lovers, who constitute the 'home' our hearts can rely on.

However, these 'homes' are both limited in space and time. They cannot be with us wherever we go, they cannot become a harbor we can rely on at all times. They cannot give our hearts the deepest permanent resting place.

In real life we walk not only amidst roses, but also amidst thorns. Our lives have, at different times, been crushed by strangers, friends or loved ones. Some people are brutally ravaged by their environment, crushed by reality, while others are injured by the people whom they love the most.

When facing of all this, some choose to indulge in desire, turn to self-pity or anger, become paralyzed, unable to move forward, waving fists at the world, while others weep late at night in the street and at sea. No matter where we cry, no matter what our situation is, we are reeds, crushed by others and crushed by ourselves.

"Man is nothing but a blade of grass, the most fragile thing in nature, but he is also a blade of grass

that can think. He is not meant to take arms against the universe with the intent to destroy it "

Life is fragile. When a deep wound is exposed, who is going to lend a helping hand? Who is the healer who bandages the deepest scars of the heart in order for us to heal? Where is the harbor deep in the soul, our truly eternal home?

"Where is our home?", we call in the depths. "I am the love, the light, the life and the road. I am what I am. If you live in me, I will live in you", a voice responds from up high.

Although we walk past the valley of the shadow of death, we are not afraid of being hurt, because His cane is supporting us. He is the lamp in front of our feet and the light that shines on the road. He set up a banquet before us when we face our enemy, and He is waiting for the prodigal son to return 'home'. Our true 'home' is buried in the depths of our spirit. It is the eternal harbor placed in our innermost being.

May you have a home deep in your heart.

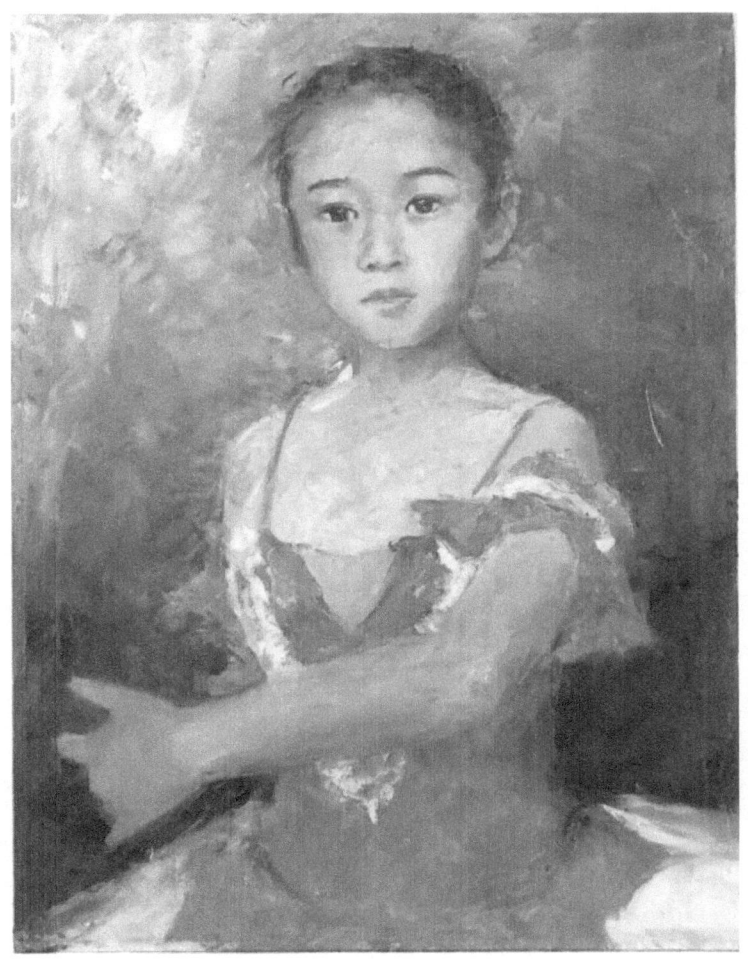

Audrey, Oil, by Jaz Xu

Journey of The Soul | Jaz Xu

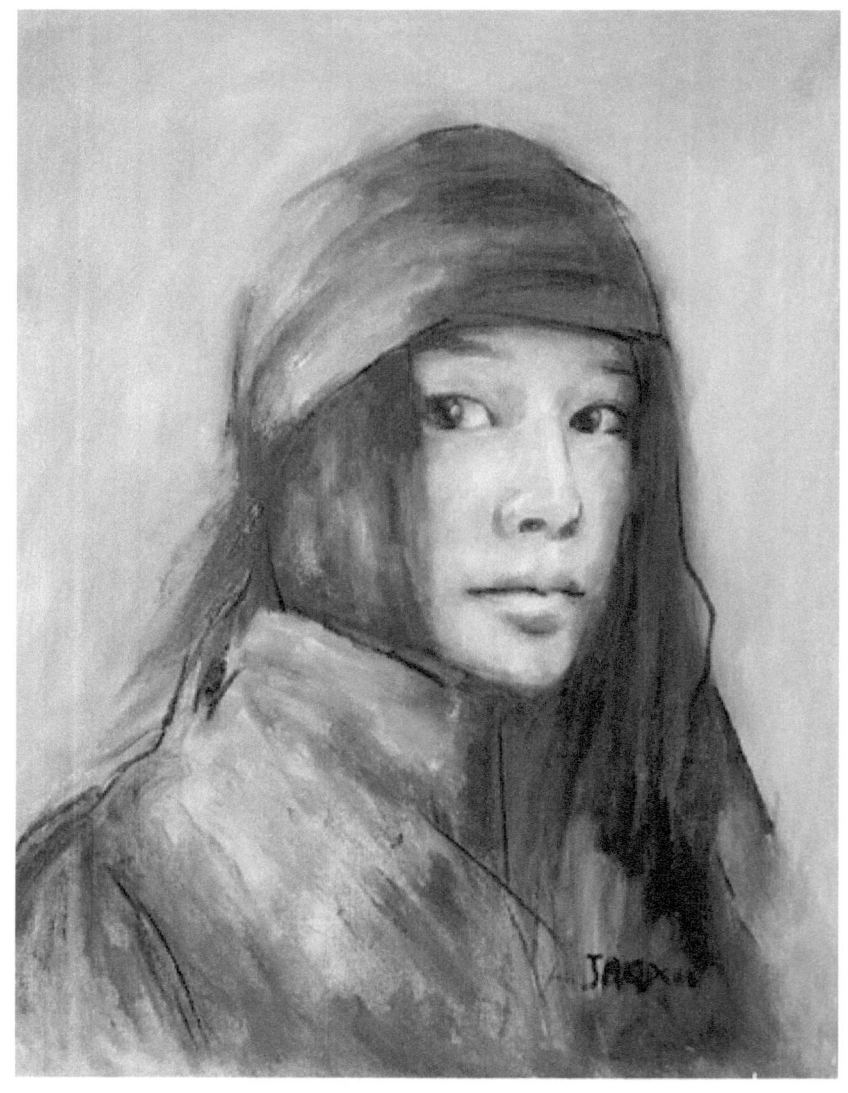

Self Portrait, Oil, by Jaz Xu

My Love Is Not In Madrid

When the afterglow of the setting sun fades, it usually heralds the beginning of a lonely, cold night. (Especially in the place I live, where people usually go to bed around 9:00 pm or 10:00 pm, even when the sky is still bright in summer). However, in Madrid, it was different. When the first light came on at dusk, Madrid, the capital city of Spain, located in the center of Spain, seemed like a sleeping giant waking up from a nap, stretching out his body and being into a motion while uttering these words with a puff: "let's get to work!" And suddenly, people started pouring into the streets and alleys, entering restaurants, bars, clubs etc., to enjoy their favorite foods, drinks, music, and other activities. A cup of sangria, a cigarette, a flamenco dance, a plate of paella, a fritter, some chocolate sauce, a slice of ham, a soccer game, Spanish people's lives had just started.

Madrid was the first stop of my trip to Spain. There was no particular reason to begin my trip there, except for the fact that Madrid was a convenient starting point for me.

When the plane landed at Madrid airport, it was already around nine o'clock in the evening. I carried my backpack, the only luggage I had for the trip, wandering around in the airport. I knew Madrid is a city where people usually sleep late, so I wasn't in a hurry to go to the hotel where I was going to stay for the night.

The high-speed rail system in Spain is one of the best in Europe, so is the public bus transport system. However, when I came out of the airport, it took me a while to look for the bus stop where I would hop on the bus which would take me to the hotel.

Spain is a nation full of passion. From the moment I landed, I felt the Spanish people's deep rooted zest for life.

"Miss, are you lost? Do you need help"? There were few people around me trying to help me when they noticed I was wandering around. I checked the map online and I was told that the bus stop was right by the exit of the airport. I went back and forth looking for the bus stop, but did not find it. I asked those people who were trying to help me where the bus stop was. When they showed it to me, to my surprise, it was right there where I stood. Why couldn't

I find it early? Maybe I had already found it, but I was not certain whether it was the right one.

The bus driver was a middle-aged man. From the time I got on the bus and told him where I was going, he kept on paying attention to me. At every stop he would tell me that we were not there yet, and the passengers around him were equally enthusiastic to make sure I wouldn't get off early.

I had to take the subway after I got off the bus (in order to really feel the life of the locals, I rarely took a taxi during the trip. I only used the public transport system). Even at around 10 o'clock at night, the Madrid subway station was still crowded. I stood in front of the ticket vending machine and struggled to buy a pass, not sure what type of pass I needed. The security guard walked a few steps towards me and helped me choose which one I should buy. He waited for me to choose the right one, so that, in case I didn't make the proper choice, he would be able to help me.

One of the important events in Madrid that summer was the World Cup. Of course, not just in Madrid. The World Cup was in full swing around the world. In Madrid, with its world famous soccer team, Real Madrid, the World Cup is a national event.

Out of the subway station, I thought I was back in China. A small store, a TV set, a group of people sitting and wearing fan costumes to watch the game there, cheering every time the ball was won or every time there was a beautiful play. Or sighing when there was a mistake. This scene was very familiar to me, just like people watching TV shows or karaoke in the streets. On the side of the road there were a lot of people who were screaming in the middle of the night. I originally thought that I would be unsafe by traveling alone. However, it seemed that this kind of worry was superfluous. At 10 o'clock in the evening, in Madrid still felt like dusk.

    The person at the hotel counter offered me the opportunity to join other guests to visit the night bars at 11pm. We would start from the first bar, would proceed to the second bar, followed by the third bar, and then we would go to the VIP nightclub at around 2am. I shook my head since I was already feeling drunk after half a glass of beer. I preferred to stay in the hotel and read. It was a very artsy hotel. Inside reds and whites everywhere. The atmosphere was lively, amiable. The style was truly unique. It was considered to be the highest-rated youth hotel in Madrid.

    My room was on the third floor and had a large window. I put my backpack down and looked out the window. An old bluestone alley, no pedestrians, not even a handsome guy holding a guitar and singing love songs to me outside the window, just a quiet night with a lonely soul. When the Taiwanese writer Sanmao was in Madrid, there was a young guy whose name was Jose used held a guitar outside of her window and sang a love song for her. For SanMao, Madrid was the place where her love started and bloomed. For me, it was the place where I could get to know Spain, experience life, and relax.

    Every time I go to a city, I like to get up early. I love to walk alone when the city is still asleep. I can feel its breath, its presence, its silence, and experience its most authentic side.

Maybe it was the reason why people sleep late at night. When I got up in the morning, the sun was already high. I hurried up and thought that I had missed a quiet time in the streets of the city. However, it was gratifying to discover that Madrid was still asleep at 8 or 9 in the morning.

Spain was a war-torn country. During the civil war, the streets of Madrid were once a battlefield. The dilapidated old wall, the ragged old slate streets live side by side with the colorful modern architecture and the asphalt covered streets. The whole city is a mix of both traditional and modern styles, markets and art. Noise and quiet coexist playfully. I walked through various streets and lanes and felt the changes brought by various historical times. Perhaps, only in the streets and lanes of Madrid could I truly feel the blending of various national cultures.

The sun shone through the cracks in the buildings, on the windows, on the porches, in the alleys, and on me. Until 10 o'clock in the morning, the shops in the city of Madrid were still closed and pedestrians were sparse. I saw some shops open the door, displaying snacks, sandwiches and other kinds of temptations. When I tried to step into them, the shopkeepers would say that they were not open yet. So it was not easy to find an open breakfast shop in the streets of Madrid at ten o'clock in the morning.

A morning trip made me feel the general atmosphere of Madrid. If I wanted to know the soul of Madrid, I needed to go deeper in order to contact it, feel it, experience it, and understand it. This couldn't be achieved in a short trip with only a few days available.

Time was limited. The only thing I could do was to get into Madrid's heart as much as possible, in order to feel her past and her present. After I returned to the hotel from the morning trip, a handsome guy at the front desk asked if I would like join five guests from all over the world to go and visit Madrid's most famous historical sites. Actually, after two hours walking the streets in the morning, I had already seen most of them in the center of Madrid. However, in order to get to know more about the city's past and contemporary life and to make acquaintance with new friends, I agreed to go with them to visit those famous sites again.

The group that I joined was made of three men and two women. When I joined them, we became three men and three women. We politely introduced ourselves to each other. Two of them were from Germany, one from Italy, one from Portugal, one from Canada and one from the US (me). There was also a guide from Portugal, a lady who worked at the hotel. She would lead us through the streets of Madrid and give us a brief description about the history of those famous sites. We wandered together, ate together, exchanged some cultural facts about our home countries, and also some information about our lives. We had a lovely time. But I knew that, in the depths of our hearts, we were alone. In Madrid, I experienced history, culture, and tasted food and wine. In fact, every dish or specialty in Madrid had historical roots. For example, the production of sangria started at the time of the plague, and the production of ham is connected with religion. On the last day, I experienced a passionate open-air concert in the city.

I read and learned a little about Madrid's history before the trip, so, every time I went to a historical site, I relived what happened in the city of Madrid by experiencing the city first hand.

Madrid was a special place for me, it gave me a very special feeling in the heart. Maybe because at first sight it made me feel like I was back in China. Maybe because of the warmth and the simple casual style of life. Maybe because of the fairytale love story of San Mao and Jose. Perhaps, in the subconscious, I too was expecting a high school student called "Jose" to sing love songs for me.

However, I knew that my true love was not in Madrid.

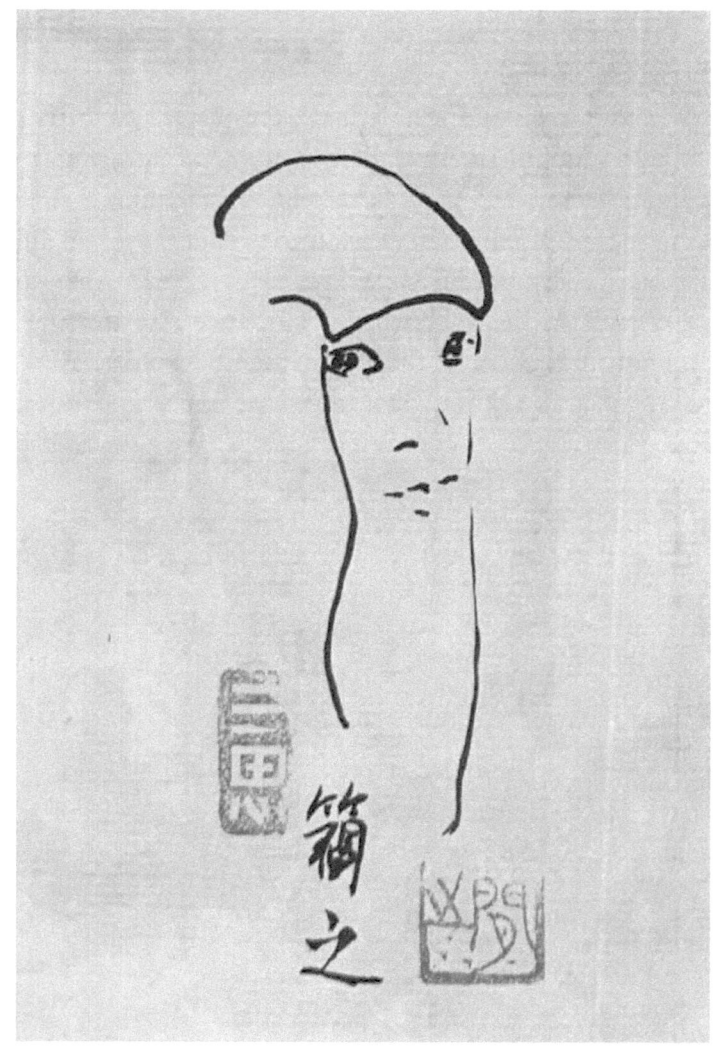

Self Portrait, Ink, by Jaz Xu

Blowing Wind

The wind blows gently,
As it brushes my face,
As it lifts my hair.
I close my eyes,
And feel your tenderness.

Journey of The Soul | Jaz Xu

I open my eyes,

To see where you come from.

Although I cannot see you,

I see the branches sway.

I know,

You exist.

The world asks

Why are there

Famine,

Death

And pain

If you're love.

You reply,

"I need to discipline."

The world asks,

"Why am I the way I am."

You say,

"The vase cannot ask the potter,

Why did you make it this way? "

In those days,

I knew,

Journey of The Soul | Jaz Xu

It had nothing to do with you,

It had to do with you,

I was falling,

In the free will you gave me.

You have been busy

You break me,

You fix me,

Because you love me.

I returned,

And left again,

I left,

And returned again,

Because you never give up.

The valley of the shadow of death,

And the absurd world,

I never fear,

Because you guard me all the time.

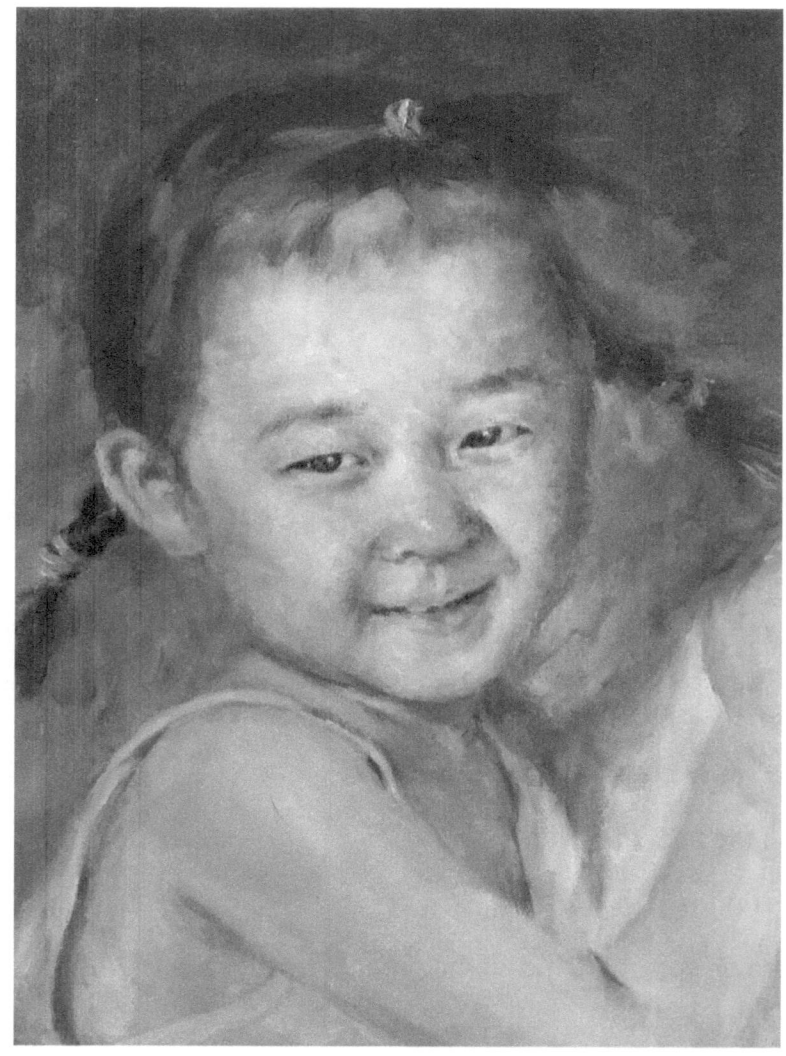

Audrey, Oil, by Jaz Xu

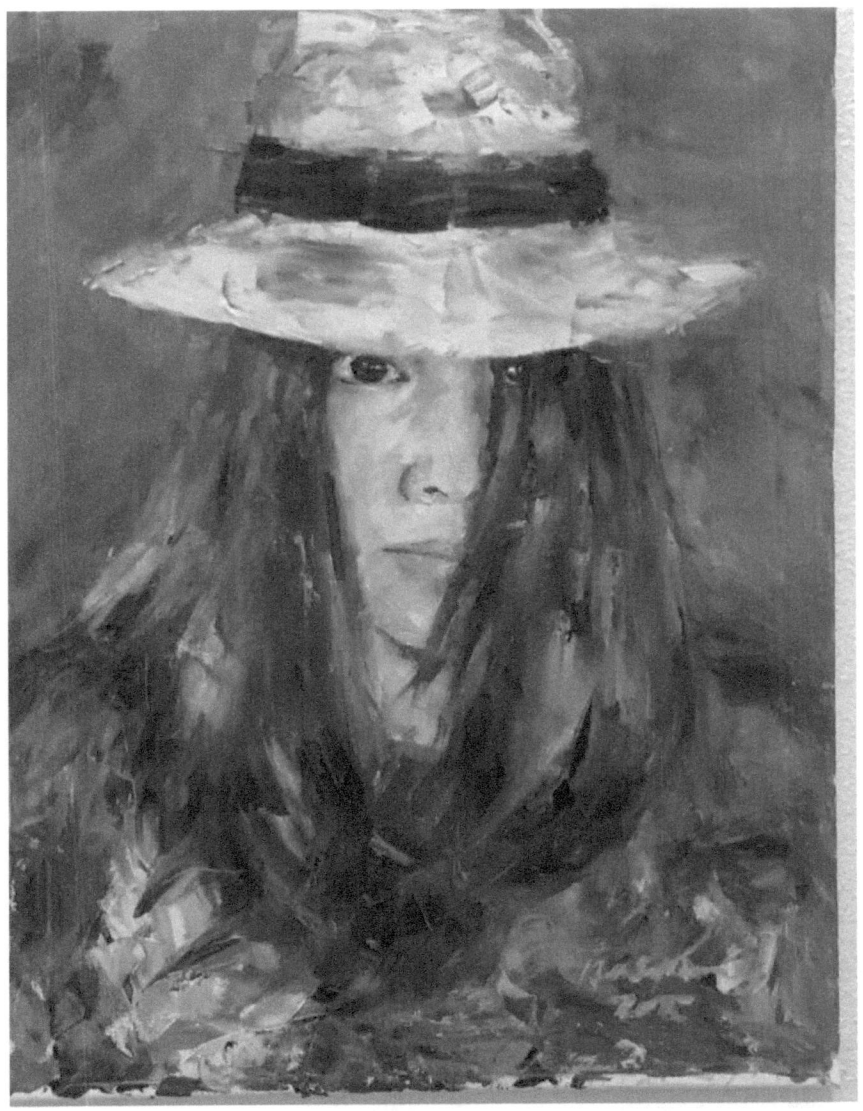

Self Portrait, Oil, by Jaz Xu

A Short Story

The night is getting darker, and the light is becoming weaker.
"Why did I give up the light for the darkness"? You were wandering among a group of people, and didn't know which direction was the right one.
"Because of love", a voice answered.
"No, love is the source of the light, but this love is against the light', you are mumbling.
Indeed, there's no eternity in the human world, nothing pure, absolute or perfect. Yet you were sinking and

seeking, until the light originally belonging to you disappeared.

What's the self? Without light, the self is nothing.

The light is shining in the darkness, and the darkness can never overcome the light.

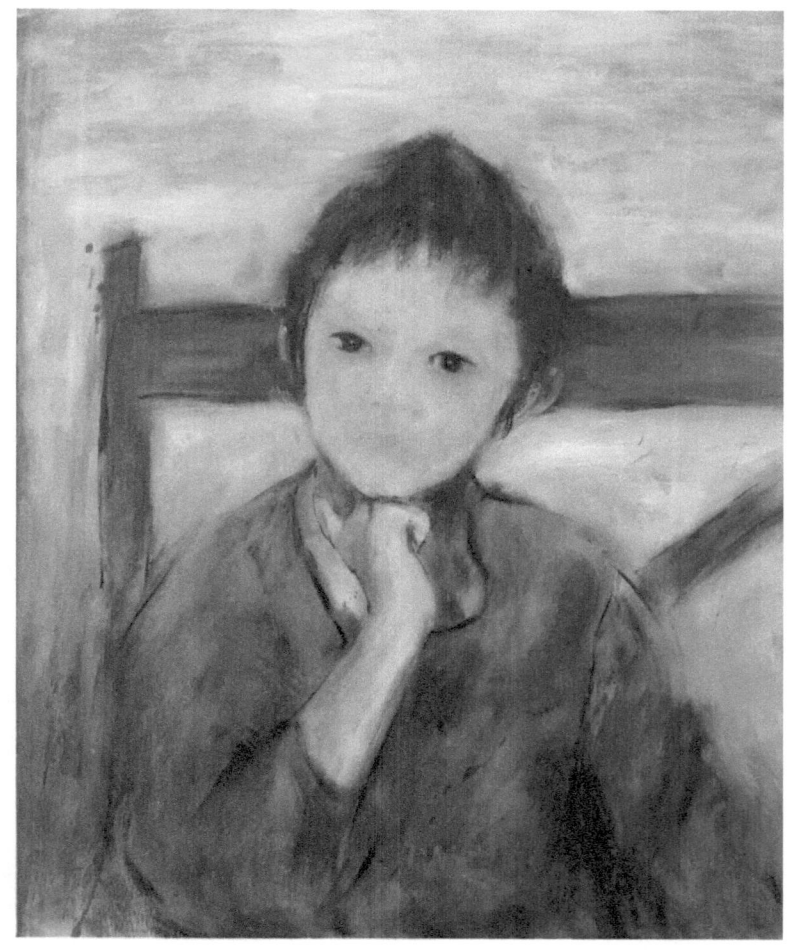

Abby, Oil, by Jaz Xu

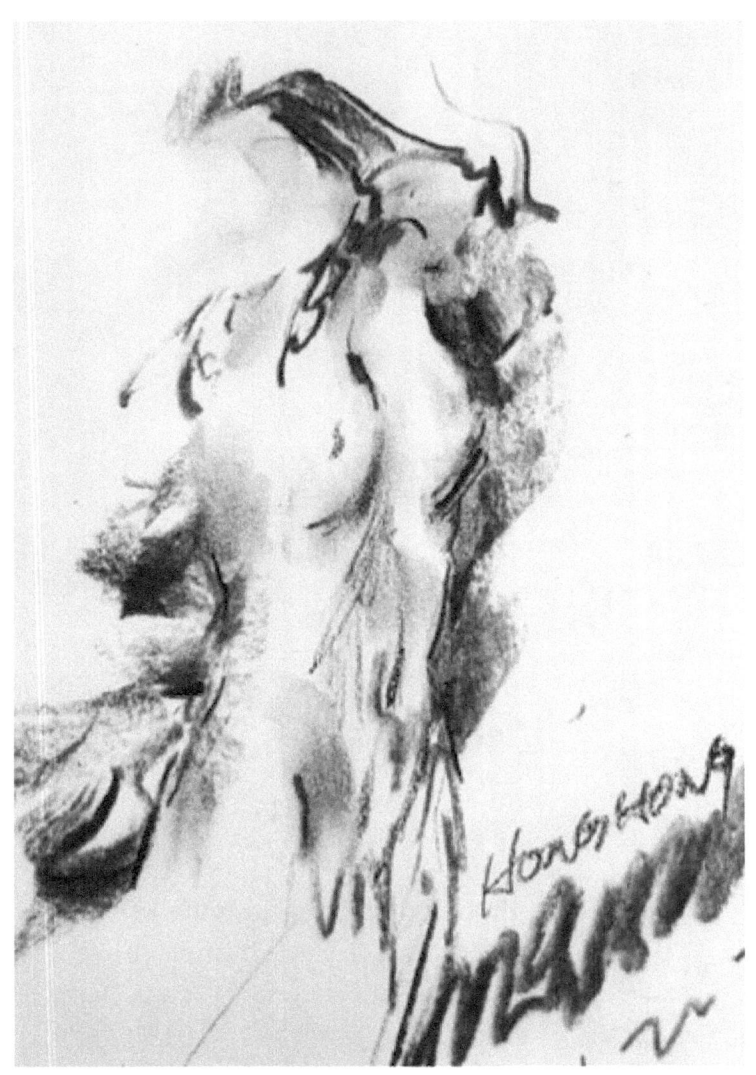

Charcoal, Jaz Xu

Jacaranda

On the first morning after arriving in South Africa, It was sunny outside of the window, and the Jacaranda trees were swaying in the sun and the breeze.

"They're amazingly beautiful!" I thought as I was looking out of the window. The purple flowers stood out under the blue sky and the white clouds, as my eyes filled with admiration.

"Jaz, do you want to go out for a walk?" Olivia, an Egyptian friend, asked me

"Isn't it dangerous"? I replied, When we arrived yesterday, James advised us not to go out, there was a 500-volt military grade fence surrounding the property. In the United States it would be against the law to use such electrified barbed wire as a fence. Maybe Olivia noticed my concern, she smiled and said: "It's pretty safe here, I just came back from a walk. If you too want to go out for a walk, I'll go with you". "It would be great! I thought people could only go out by car. If we can go out for a walk, that will be a really big prize for me. "I put on my hat and followed Olivia.

Once we went out of the courtyard through a big iron door, I was immediately immersed in the light fragrance of the blue purple Jacaranda flowers. On both sides of the street there were rows of Jacaranda trees with purple and blue flowers drifting around. I looked up and gazed for a while. My mind went blank, as I could only utter the words: "So beautiful!".

With every step, I exclaimed "Really beautiful"! Whether it was the purple flowers covering the ground, or the brown and dark branches graced by blue and purple, they all touched my heart deeply. In particular, when the breeze was blowing and blue waves gently swayed overhead, I stopped and let the blue flowers flutter all around me. I said: "Flowers bloom and fly all over the sky". I relished the feeling, as I forgot where I was.

"Actually, the most beautiful time is the time when the green leaves of Jacaranda gradually fall, as they are replaced by blooming purple flowers" Olivia said as we were walking.

"It's so beautiful", I sighed again, and repeatedly looked up and down, as my head filled with blue-purple dreams.

Pretoria is known as the garden city. October is the most beautiful season. The city is famous for its beautiful purple flowers tunnels. They say there are over 70,000 trees forming these tunnels which grace the city. As I was walking that small street, the blue flowers had me completely intoxicated.

"Hi good morning, how are you?", Olivia greeted strangers who passed by while we were walking on the street. "Here, strangers often talk to each other", she said. I felt like telling her that in North America people do the same.

On the street, we occasionally crossed groups of two or three people, walking quietly. In the sun, in the breeze, under the blue sway, we were walking and talking.

"What countries have you visited?", Olivia asked me.

"Not many. I have been to a few countries in Europe and Asia. Naturally North America, and now I am here in South Africa." I answered.

"Of all the places you visited, which one is your favorite one?", she continued.

"I liked Toledo in Spain, Bath in the UK, and some small towns in France". I was thinking of my favorite cities and towns, and realized that what I really liked were actually the medieval buildings designed according to ancient Rome's style. These cities retain Roman architecture, art and culture. Of course, there were many cities I haven't yet been to, but they were on my list of places to visit.

"And you? Which is your favorite place?", I asked Olivia.

"I love traveling. Australia is the place I liked the most. The natural scenery is so beautiful there, and I am particularly attracted to natural beauty. In the near future, I'm planning to go to visit Asian and African countries." She answered.

Actually, I would like to tell her, for me every place I visited or I will be visiting is home, I hope my feet could take me to every corner of the world. In every trip I enjoy meeting with local people. I fall in love with a city because I truly fall in love with the people who live there.

"Have you ever been to the Middle East?", Olivia asked me.

"Not yet", I replied.

"If you go to the Middle East, you'll be captivated, and I'm sure you'll love so many things there". Olivia's eyes sparkled when she was talking about her native land. Just as my eyes must have sparkled when I was talking about China.

"Can I talk to you for a second?". Under the blue flowers, an elegant old lady with silver hair came toward us and stopped in front of us, holding an Old Testament book in her hand. Beside her stood a smartly dressed handsome gentleman.

We stopped to listen to her quietly. She opened the Old Testament and pointed to a verse which she proceeded to read to us. Her face was filled with joy.

"You're a Jehovah's witness, aren't you?" Olivia asked after she finished the reading. The lady nodded and Olivia proceeded to say: "We believe in Lord Jesus Christ, the Son of God, who died for our sins, and was reborn as the life giving spirit which we can receive as our salvation. We are saved and reborn by accepting His spirit of life, which is the eternal life, and this is our belief." While listening to Olivia's firm words, I sensed that the elegant old lady's face had changed, and the original luster had disappeared. There was an awkward look on her face because of the challenge she got from Olivia.

"Thank you for sharing, it's time for us to go back." I smiled at her shyly, hoping to limit her embarrassment.

"Have you believed in the Lord for a long time?" I asked Olivia on the way back.

"I grew up going to a traditional church, but it was only two years ago that I really started to know the truth. At that time Egypt had restored church life, and I really felt that God was my Lord", Olivia replied. She continued: "Our Lord is God and Spirit, and one day God will let the Jehovah's Witnesses know that Jesus is God the Lord." Her tone was full of strength.

Two years of understanding gave birth to such firm confidence, and formed such solid foundation. Many people who say they believe in the Lord not necessarily get to know the Lord in their lifetime, and they're unable to take a firm stand behind their own beliefs. Their beliefs are like seeds sprinkled on rocks, shallow soil, or thorny bushes. If the wind's direction changes, the beliefs will also follow, bending like reeds. The mouth says the Lord's name, but the heart is far away from the Lord. Of course that was also a reminder to myself.

On the way back to the residence, still walking amidst trees full of beautiful blue and purple, I looked up to praise the Creator of the blue flowers, the Creator of all things in the universe: You are the all-encompassing one, You are subject, but You are also the object. You are science (scientists have only discovered the science You created) and You are also a philosopher (philosophers only understand and sum up Your laws in the universe, such as LaoZi).

You are the light in the darkness, and the darkness never overcomes you.

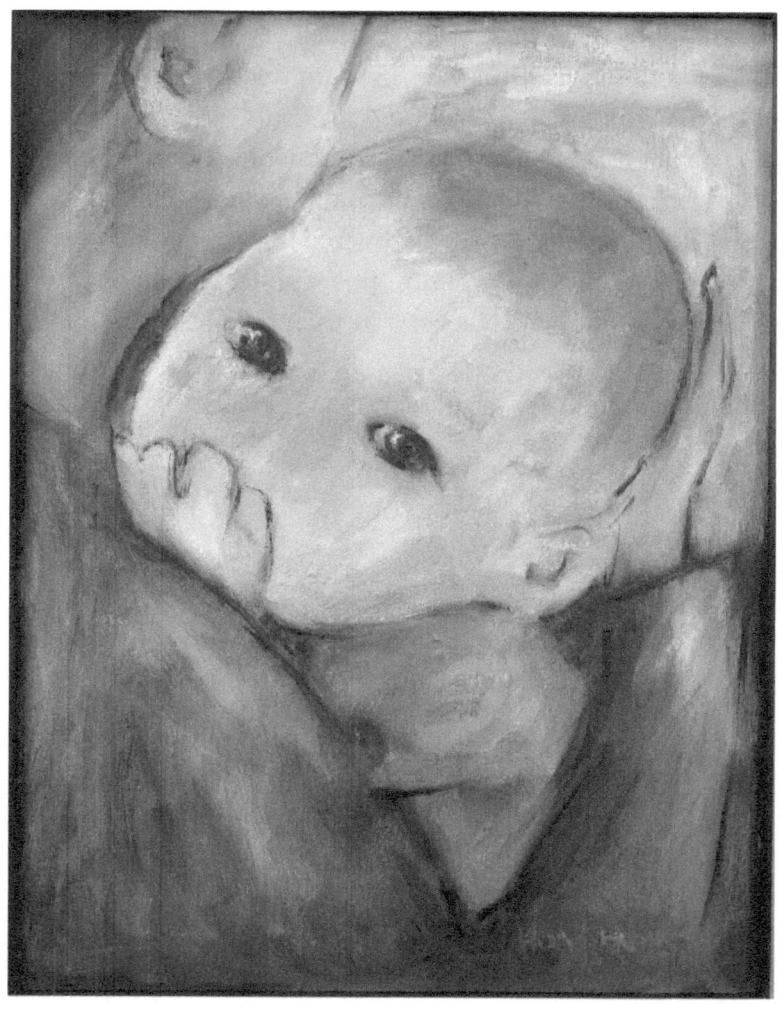

Innocent, Oil, by Jaz Xu

The Diamond Life

When my friend mentioned that we were going to visit the diamond mine, I wasn't too excited, since I didn't care much about diamonds. However, I was willing to learn about diamond mining from a historical and cultural perspective. The famous Cullinan diamond, the so called "Star of Africa," was mined in South Africa. South Africa is famous for its diamond and gold mines.

Although I do not love jewelry, if I were forced to choose a precious gemstone, I would choose diamonds. A diamond not only is the world famous symbol of true love, but it also has a crystal clear, sparkling and flawless external appearance.

When we arrived, Cullinan appeared to be a small town, much smaller than I had thought, but it was neat and elegant. Obviously, the diamond mine in that town was also very different from what I imagined.

After the bus stopped, I was still unsure where the famous Cullinan diamond mine was actually located. I spotted a small wooden house hidden under a tall banana tree. I took several photos of the entrance door, and asked a staff who welcomed us "Is this the diamond mine"? "Yes, it is", he replied. I went inside full of curiosity, but I was more curious about the tourists' observation room than about the mine. We were asked to put on a helmet before watching the information video. Thereafter we would be visiting the mine.

The video documented the mine's history and the diamond mining process. We were lead to visit the actual mine. The video taught us that some mines have five shafts, each one kilometer long, and that there is a community living in each shaft, deep underground. I marveled at the determination, perseverance and intelligence of humanity when it comes to claiming wealth from nature. When the staff described the method used to find a diamond from hard kimberlite and the process to turn a piece of rough diamond into a crystal clear shiny diamond, I was equally amazed at the technology and professional skills required to mill diamonds.

I was thinking that diamonds are a bit like humans, they need to be changed and honed.

I thought about myself, I was also a piece of kimberlite, and I also have a diamond inside – my spirit, together with the Holy Spirit are in me in the same way as diamonds are inside kimberlite.

This 'honed' spirit represents my true life force. As it grows inside, it spreads to my soul and my body. This process of life growing and manifesting itself outside is like a kimberlite being smashed, the diamond inside being milled, cut, polished, finally revealing a flawless, crystal clear gemstone. Human nature needs to be broken, cut, grown and ground, to finally become pure, flawless, vital energy.

When diamonds are found underground, they are in a primitive shape, valuable, yes, but rough (as in the idiomatic expression: a diamond in the rough). When diamonds are turned into jewelry, they are transformed by the work and craftsmanship of humans. Similarly, when we accept the Holy Spirit as the essence of the divine element of life, we find that there is a treasure inside our earthly shell, but this treasure needs to infiltrate us, become a major component of our existence. It also needs to be manifested outside.

To accomplish this work puts us in direct contact with the Universe, as the past, present and future all become manifestations of the eternal God. God becomes the spirit of life diffused into our spirit, as it affects and changes us, the gift of divine life which spreads from the inside all the way to our whole body, as we finally turn into "diamonds". Every time I think about it, I am moved and feel like praising the one who's above: what a blessing this is! I am the work of the Creator of the Universe, and God is the artist who wants to make my life pure and complete.

What other thing in this world is more valuable than being the work of God, a perfected human being? Moreover, I am not only the work of God, but I am also the instrument of God, as I am imbued with divine spirit. God himself is my real joy, as He nourishes my true needs in the depths of my soul.

God is my source of wisdom and love. The formation of a perfect diamond requires high temperature, high pressure, time and nutrients. Figuratively so, each of our lives requires the same. And I called this 'diamond life'.

Self Portrait, Oil, by Jaz Xu

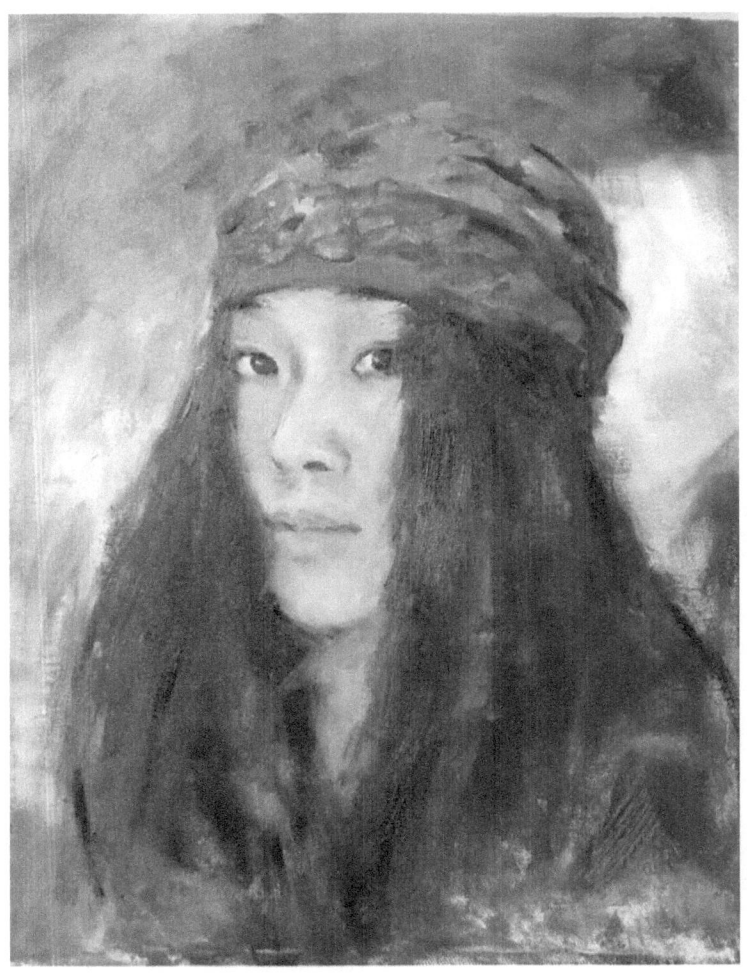

My Art Journey

The road is long and goes far away, I will search it up and down. I call myself an art explorer. As I walk along that road, I progress slowly but steadily.

Being able to devote myself to artistic creation has been for me a way to feel happiness and joy in the very depths of my heart. Being an artist is a happy profession, because it is a profession that deals with 'self'. No matter how busy the world is, the artist can always live in a constant state of elation. The artist can freely express the deepest elements of her soul, her most authentic emotions, in the purest possible way. Sometimes, I find myself not having communicated with anyone all day, but, in the process of creation, I can 'talk' with my own creations, the characters floating on the canvas. This communication is unfiltered and complete. Sometimes, when I am moved by looking at the eyes of the characters painted on the canvas, I can cry without any embarrassment. At that moment my soul experiences a full union with its creation.

Being authentic is my art. No matter what technique or method I use, I express the aspects of my soul in the most authentic way. The emotions are transferred to the canvas in the purest form. No matter how technological, conceptualized, fashionable, trendy, commercialized, materialized, vulgarized, exaggerated and falsified in the throngs of the conventional world, Truth is the root and essence of my art. Truth has a powerful beauty of its own. It does not refer to an external object, but it derives an instinctual, most authentic, purest power directly from its source: human nature. The power associated with this beauty can be shocking. When I see that the viewers are deeply touched by my art, as tears of joy stream deep down inside their hearts, it is the moment when I can fully appreciate the extent of success achieved in the process of creating art.

The artwork originates from the creator's own inner world. Its manifestation cannot deceive people. People can easily perceive how true the artist is through the authenticity of her art; how clear the artist is, through the clarity of her art, and how deep the artist's soul is, through the depth of her art. Art is the inner world of the artist. In the artist's work one finds purity, depth, clarity, vision, as long as these are the qualities of the artist herself.

By examining some of my art produced in the past, I have discovered the road ahead, as it appears to me: long and clear. No matter how the world changes, how fashions and trends come and go, my art is always consistent. Despite the changes, the works of art are firmly attached to their own origins, by describing the truth, by giving humanity a chance to discover the deep charm within, by expressing the most authentic emotions, by igniting life itself. Pure light.

It's a long way to go, but I'll walk steadily with joy in my heart.

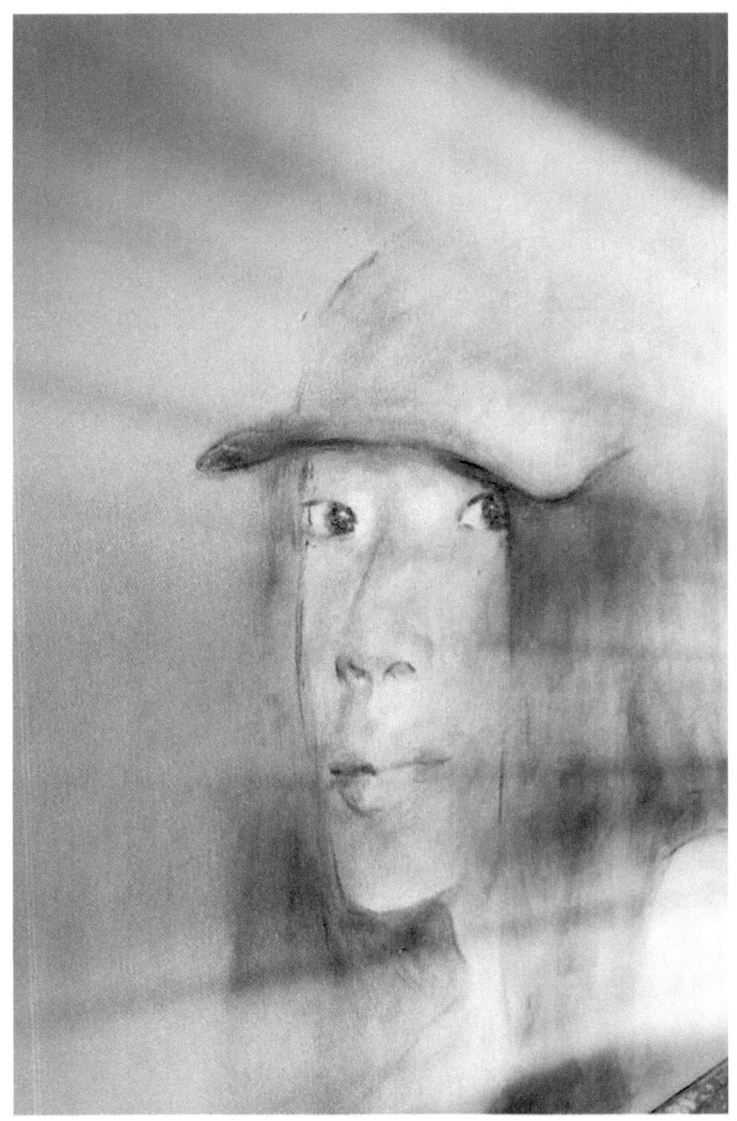

Self Portrait, Oil, by Jaz Xu

Promise

God hath not promised skies always blue,
Flower-Strewn pathways all our lives through;
God hath not promised sun without rain,
Joy without sorrow, peace without pain.
But God hath promised strength for the day,
Rest from the labor, light for the way,
Grace for the trials, help from above,
Unfailing sympathy, and undying love.

Indeed, because of the light of life, because of the power of the supporting, unfailing compassion and undying love from God, we can stand up again after falling into temptation. Helped by His never-ending love and support, we can leave the crowds and live in the Lord peacefully.

Without God's love, it's hard to get to know ourselves better, have peace in adversity, and still love the one who betrayed us.

It's right (wrong), and you should do this (that): this is the common phenomenon of people's judgments and demands, no matter what their background may be. I always hear people asking, "How could a Christian do this type of things?" People love to judge others as well as being judged by others. People guard against others as well as they love being guarded by others. Even a person like a Christian, without God's presence and revelation, will also become judgmental.

However, there are some good examples of people who are always at peace and manage to love others no matter what the situation. They are not consumed by self-pity or in search of excuses, but instead enjoy God's presence and love. They're lifted, and face fights, scams, and cheats in a peaceful way.

People who believe in God are sinners receiving grace. Because of our imperfection, we are willing to be transformed. And because of God's presence, each failure in our life becomes our gift from Him. The purpose of believing in God isn't just simply to try to be a good man doing good deeds, but it is also to try to have one's life deep inside transformed and developed, as it manifests itself in our daily activities. We don't just praise the graces received from God, but we also appreciate all the unfavorable situations we encounter and know that everything is in His hands and that we are supported by

Him. We are given grace, but we are also broken down, rebuilt and disciplined by God.

I myself am easily provoked, and I hate to be cheated. I like to argue with people who misunderstand me, and I try to clear things out and make people understand me. However, God is wisdom. He makes me know no one is perfect in this world except Himself, but even though the Himself is perfect, He is still misunderstood, betrayed, forced to wear a crown of thorns, abused, cast aside, and put on the cross. Not even to mention us, the imperfect humans. Therefore, I learned to release the negative emotions caused by being misunderstood, and turn to the Lord wherever there is a failure or a hint of depression. The moment I turn to the Lord, the moment for myself to be broken and rebuilt, and which makes my life starts to grow.

Whenever our hearts turn to the Lord, the veil is taken away. The universal creator is the Christ but it is also a mystery, the spirit we experience and enjoy, the direction of our life, the lamp in front of our feet, the light on our journey. *Even though we walk through the valley of the shadow of death, but we will never be afraid since He is with us, His rod and His staff comfort us.*

God's promises never fail, and He never forgets His eternal covenant: God lives in man, and man lives in God.

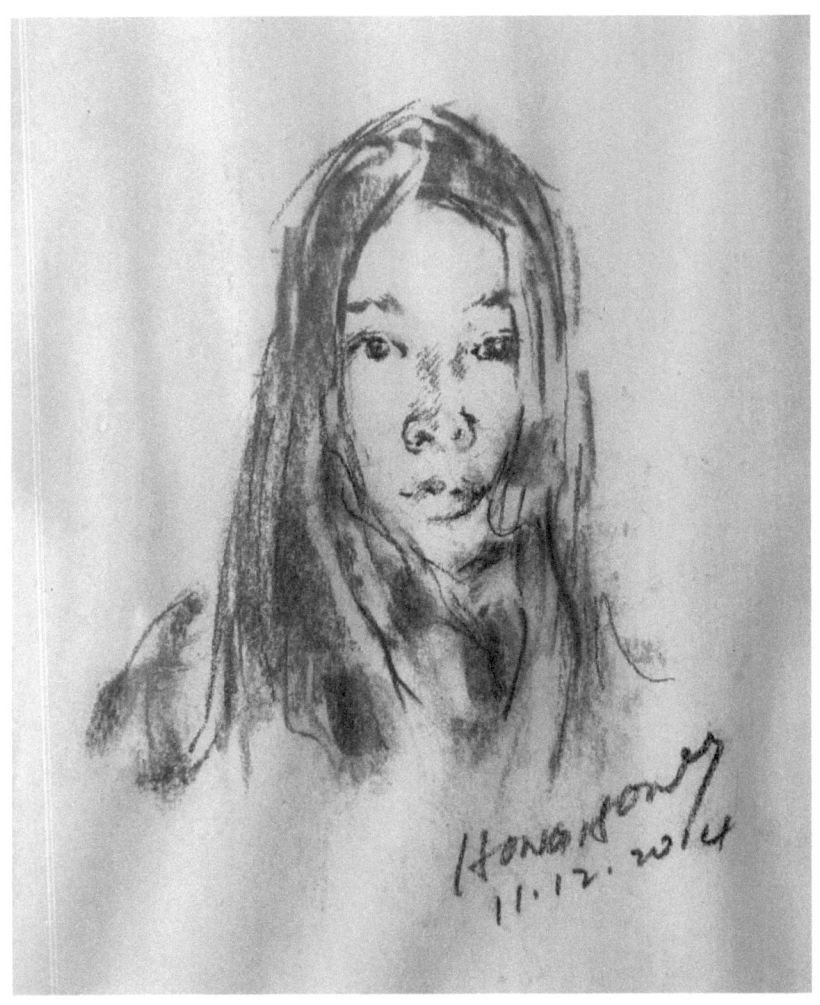

Self Portrait, Charcoal, by Jaz Xu

Journey of The Soul | Jaz Xu

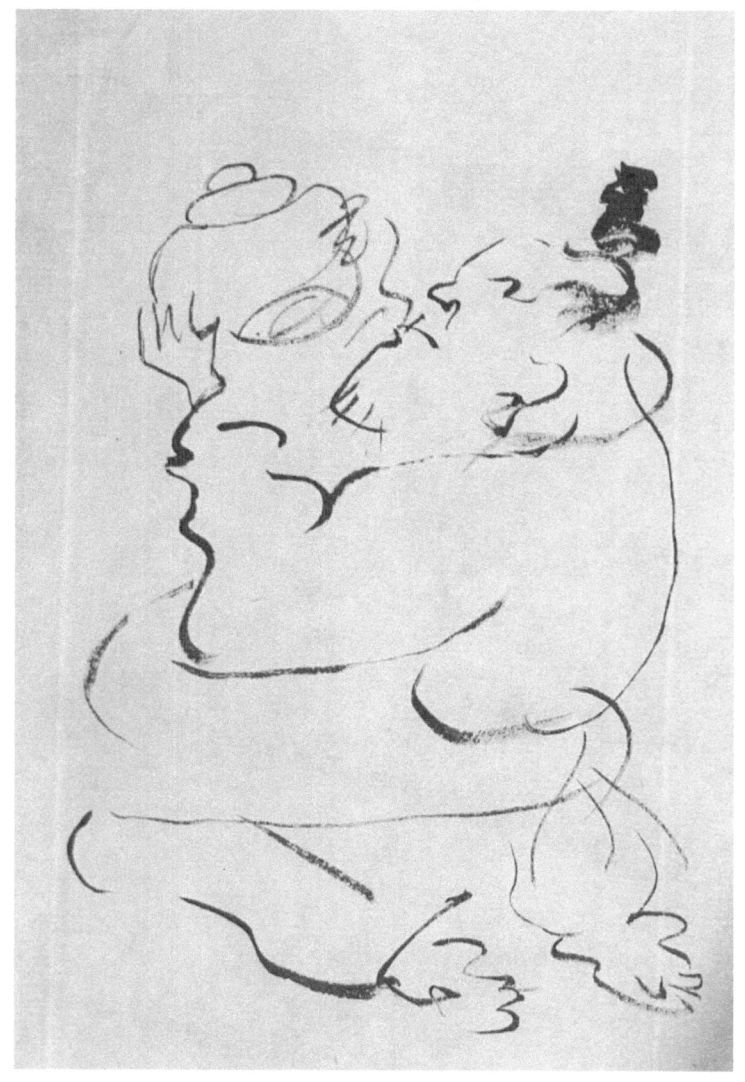

Drinking, Ink, by Jaz Zu

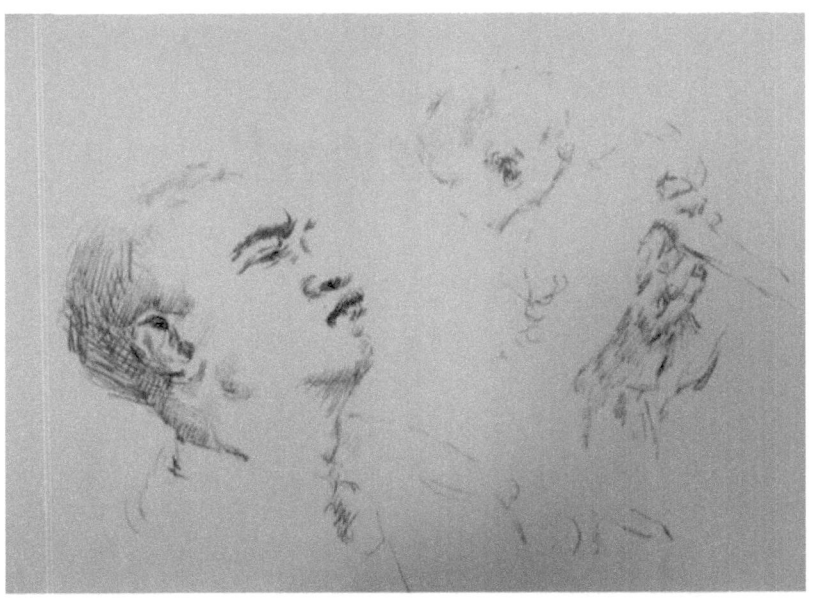

Love, Pen, by Jaz Xu

Loving Yourself

A few days ago, I went to the house of a friend whom I just met. There was a mail truck parked in front of her house, as dozens of parcels lied on the ground in front of her door. I was surprised, entered the door and asked, "Did you buy all this stuff?" "It's S's." Her husband replied. I helped carry the parcels into the house.

However, after entering the door, I was even more surprised when I saw that the aisle was full of online shopping boxes, like a warehouse. "What's going on here?" I asked her again, out of curiosity. "They are clothes, shoes and other things which have been purchased, and some are ready to be returned.", was the reply. I said nothing. When I entered the living room, I discovered there were more than a dozen expensive bags, dozens of expensive shoes.

"Are these all yours"? I asked again. I became even more curious.

"Yes, these are for resale, and there are even more that have already been resold".

"Why did you buy so many if you do not intend to keep them"? I asked.

"We should love ourselves. If you don't love yourselves, who else will love you"? she replied.

Love yourself, you can find this expression in many articles about chicken soup. When one hears these words, they sound very reasonable. They have become the guide for many people's thinking and behavior. Indeed, we need to love ourselves. But does it really mean 'to love oneself'? What is the most important thing in our life?

I know that all these objects satisfy her material desires, give her a brief moment of happiness, resulting in the illusion that she loves herself. However, these material possessions didn't bring her real happiness and psychological health, and didn't bring her peace after conflicts with relatives and loved ones. I believe that this is not only her problem, but the problem of the people of all kinds.

What's the proper way to love yourself? To love yourself is to cherish your body, soul, and spirit.

Because of your love for yourself, you protect your own body from harm, you avoid eating and drinking mindlessly, you try not to stay up too late and become excessively tired, you try to avoid doing anything that could be harmful to your health. Because of the love for your body, you try to control desires and try to avoid treating your body mindlessly.

To love yourself, you also should love your own soul. Treat all world's affairs with a tolerant, generous heart. Love yourself by making your soul happy and content.

Many things in this multicolored world can give people a temporary high, but then, what happens afterwards? When the night falls and everything goes silent, don't you fell inside an unspoken sense of emptiness flowing through your whole body?

The multitude of thoughts, the confusion created by money, what comes out of all this? The answer comes from a passage in the Bible, "The broken spirit dries up the bones". The true love of yourself, the one that makes you constantly happy, comes from deep inside, from the love and awe of the highest life, from the enjoyment of the most sacred Holy Spirit.

To 'love yourself' also means to love your own 'real' life. "What good is it if a man earns the world and loses his soul's life?" (Matthew 16:26). What else can one exchange for his soul? How does a man who doesn't even love his life love himself?

There is nothing wrong with someone satisfying the survival needs of his own body in order to keep alive. But true love for life is not just about keeping your body alive. The life of the body is a short, shallow life, limited, for the majority of people, to less than a hundred years span. But the real love for one's life is the love for the 'real' life, that is, the spiritual life.

Some people that are alive are act already dead, while others are truly alive. Because of the original sin, we experience death. This death is not the death of the body, but the death of spiritual life. In order to cherish our lives, we need to let our spiritual life last forever: this is not only the hope of man but it is also God's promise.

"For God so loved the world that He gave His one and only Son, that whoever believes in Him shall not perish but have eternal life." (John 3:16)

Perhaps you don't realize that the fact that you don't accept divine life will make death a terrible thing to endure, and you get comfort from thinking that everyone will die anyway. But what I want to tell you is that although people experience the same physical death, the end of life is not the same for all.

According to the prophecy of the bible (the bible is the living book of life. It is also a book of prophecies, of which more than 90 percent have come true, while the rest will soon come true) : "And I saw the dead, great and small, standing before the throne, and books were opened. Another book was opened, which is the book of life. The dead were judged according to what they had done as recorded in the books. The sea gave up the dead that were in it, and death and Hades gave up the dead that were in them, and each person was judged according to what they had done. Then death and Hades were thrown into the lake of fire. The lake of fire is the second death. Anyone whose name was not found written in the book of life was thrown into the lake of fire" (Revelation 20:12).

"Then I saw 'a new heaven and a new earth,' for the first heaven and the first earth had passed away, and there was no longer any sea" (Revelation 21:1). "He will wipe every tear from their eyes. There will be no more death or mourning or crying or pain, for the old order of things has passed away" (Revelation 21:4).

These are the things that humans will have to face in the future, no matter how your body dies, it is really all about the end of your spiritual life.

So, real love for yourself consists of cherishing your own life, accepting the eternal highest life, the one given by God. Enjoy the divine spirit and become fully satisfied. "A happy heart is the medicine." Let the deepest joy in the spirit extend through your soul to reach your body.

Love yourself, cherish the spiritual life, cherish the soul, cherish the body. The highest love is the love for the one who is the creator of this universe, the love for His will, the love for what He loves, and the love received from Him. Without the love of the Lord, we cannot ever love ourselves, for the Lord knows us better than we do.

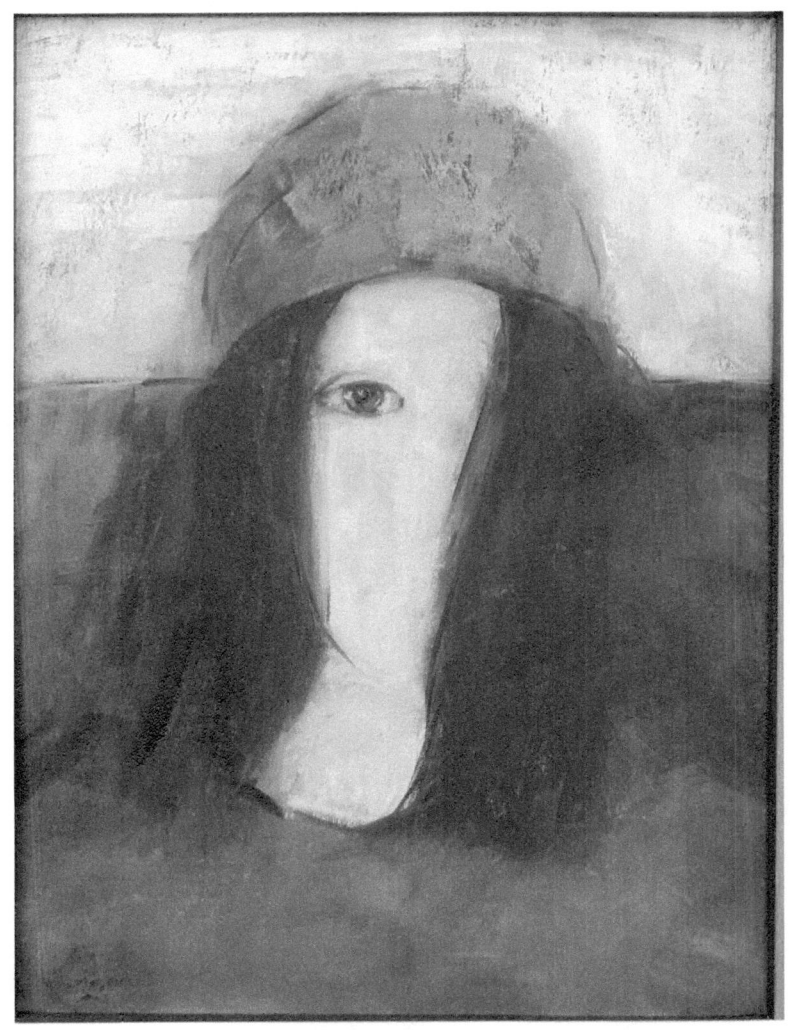

Self Portrait, Oil, by Jaz Xu

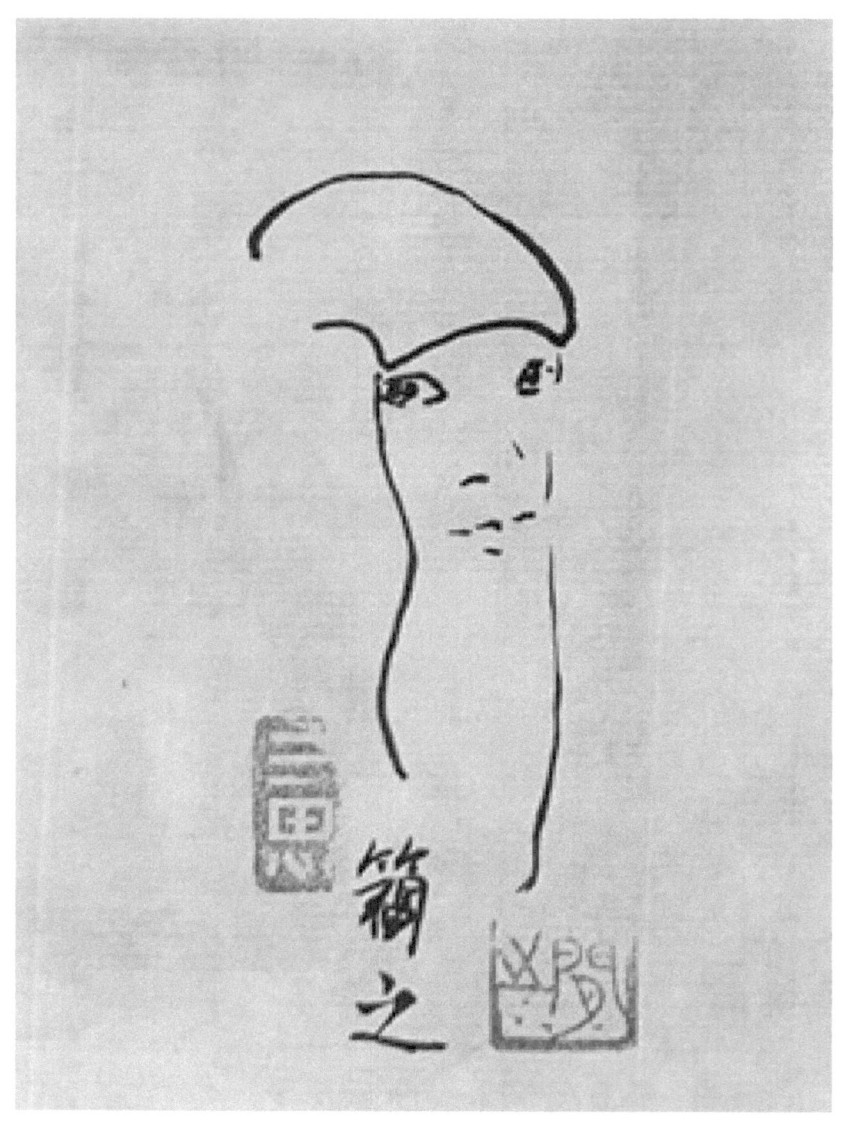

Sketch, ink, by Jaz Xu

Journey of The Soul | Jaz Xu

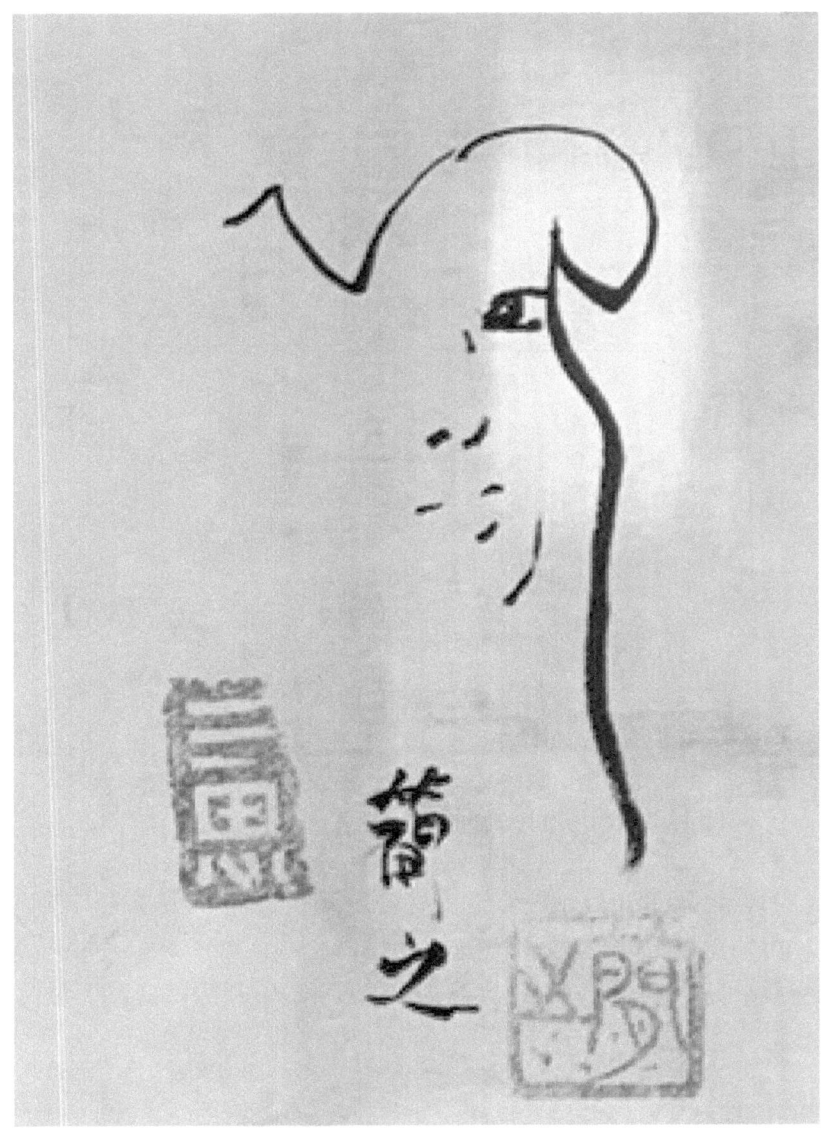

Self Portrait, ink, by Jaz Xu

A Story Of The Past

Yesterday morning, when I thought about a crazy thing in the previous year once more, fifteen years had already been past.

That winter, F was in a full-time training in Cleveland Ohio, and I was in Toronto Canada to clean up some of our staffs. I clearly remembered it was a snowing day, heavy snow. Suddenly, I felt I missed him so much as I was watching the snowflakes flying up and down. I got rid of the things I was working on immediately and prepared to visit him.

The snow was getting heavier, but I was full of enthusiasm, "I'm going to visit him, and giving him a big surprise!" I was full of energy.

My car was covered by a layer of heavy snow. I opened the trunk and took out the snow brush to clean the windows. F was calling in.

"What are you doing now"? He asked.

"Nothing, I want to go out." I replied carefully to prevent being suspected by him.

"Where are you going? Is it snowing over there"? He asked with care, but full of worries. He is a type of person easy to worry.

"nothing special, it's snowing here, but not so heavy, and I'm going to go to the library." I was lying. Every time, when I was trying to go someplace where I didn't want him to know, I would say I'm going to the library. Not sure, whether he was suspicious. "Anyway, I'm going to give him a big surprise, so I'll never ever let him suspect me". I murmured to myself. I was imaging about the moment when he saw me with full of surprise, and I was so excited. I was encouraged by myself.

"Safe drive". His voice full of caring, but more of worry.

"Don't worry, nothing will be happened, I'm a good driver". I grinned secretly.

It took at least two hours from Toronto to the USA border. From my past experiences, it would take about six hours from Toronto to Cleveland in a normal weather day, but it was a heavy snowing day, not sure whether it would take longer hours. However, I was so in the mood of giving him the surprise, therefore, nothing difficult will stop me.

Maybe the heaven was moved by my brave and enthusiasm, the snow wasn't stop, but instead, becoming heavier. There was a truck cleaning the snow on the street and sprinkling the salt on top of it. The road was ok to drive, for my speed was almost the same as usual.

I was speeding on the road, while sing the song only myself could understand, and meanwhile, imaging the scenery after F saw me, I was so moved by myself.

Out of car windows, was a white world. It was a beautiful field any time during the year. I love to drive on the road which connects Canada and USA, since it's beautiful in all seasons, and I love to look at those beautiful views while driving. Usually, F was the one drive, so I had more time to look at those beautiful idyllic landscape which always touches me.

Though, it was a snow stormy day, maybe because only few cars on the road, or maybe because I drove too fast, it took me less hours than usual to arrive at the border.

"where do you live? What's your purpose of coming to USA"? the officer at the customs asked.

"From Toronto, and to see my husband". I replied.

"Driving alone in this type of weather"? The motion on officer's face was complicate.

"Yes". My answer was firm and joy.

Maybe, the officer was moved by my great action as well. He let me pass quickly. I kept driving right after adding more gasoline and finishing the restroom. I didn't waste a second for the stop.

No mater it was because of love or just the curious about how F reaction would be after seeing me, anyway, it was my first time driving six hours alone, and on a snow stormy day. However, it was the new beginning for my future road trip.

I was passing one car and another, I was so proud of myself. "I could do anything if I want," I was feeling smug. "calm down" I remind myself. I tried to be calm and continue to image the moment when F saw me. Will he be excited? Giggling? Or hugging me up and circling? I had many imaged sceneries but the real one.

When I knocked the door of the house, a brother from the church opened it for me. When I asked where F was, he pointed to one of the bedrooms. I knocked on the bedroom door, it opened itself since it was ajar. F was lying in the bed. He was up a little bit and smiling to me when seeing me and continuing lying back to sleep. I stood there, I felt cold. I had so many imagines about what his reaction would be but none liked this.

I stood there silently while F was still in bed. Brother from the church saw me was still standing at the door, and he felt strange. "Your wife is here." He called F. Suddenly, F got out of the bed. "When did you get here? I don't know the one stand there was you since I didn't see very clearly without my glasses on." Well he was surprised when he noticed it was me, but far beyond what I imagined.

We love to live in a way we would expect, however, life doesn't always satisfy you based on what we want, instead it'll give you something beyond what you expect. Sometimes, it's joy. Sometimes, it's pity. Overall, It's wonderful.

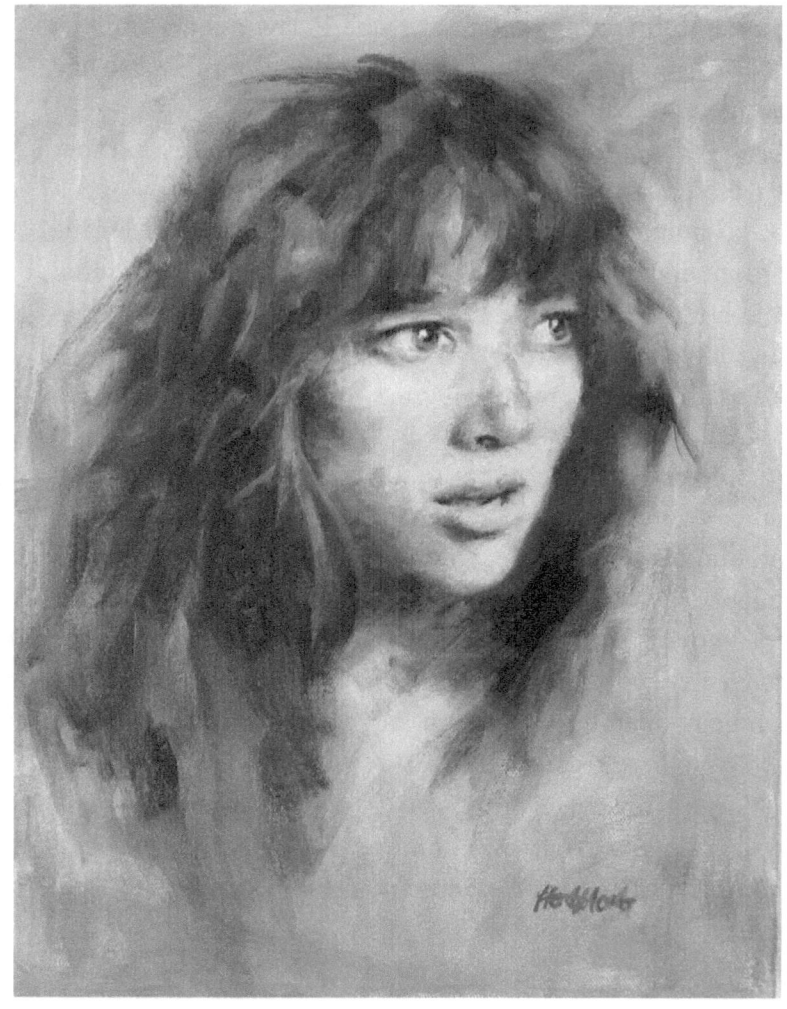

Oil, by Jaz Xu

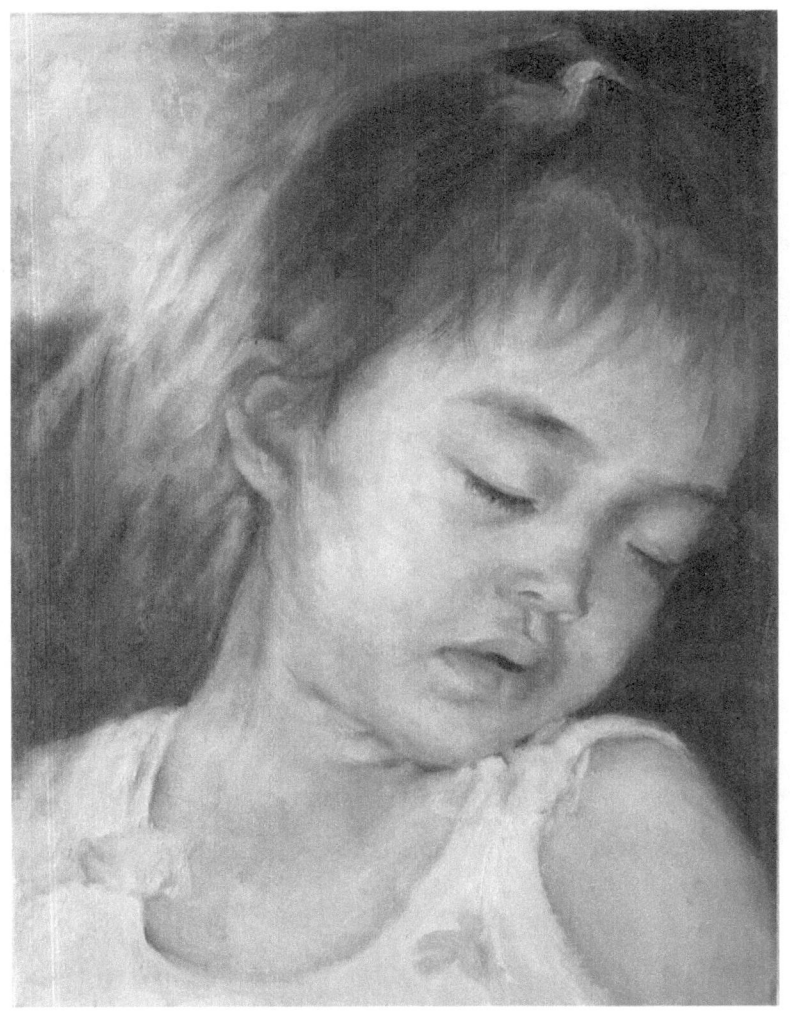

Abby, Oil, by Jaz Xu

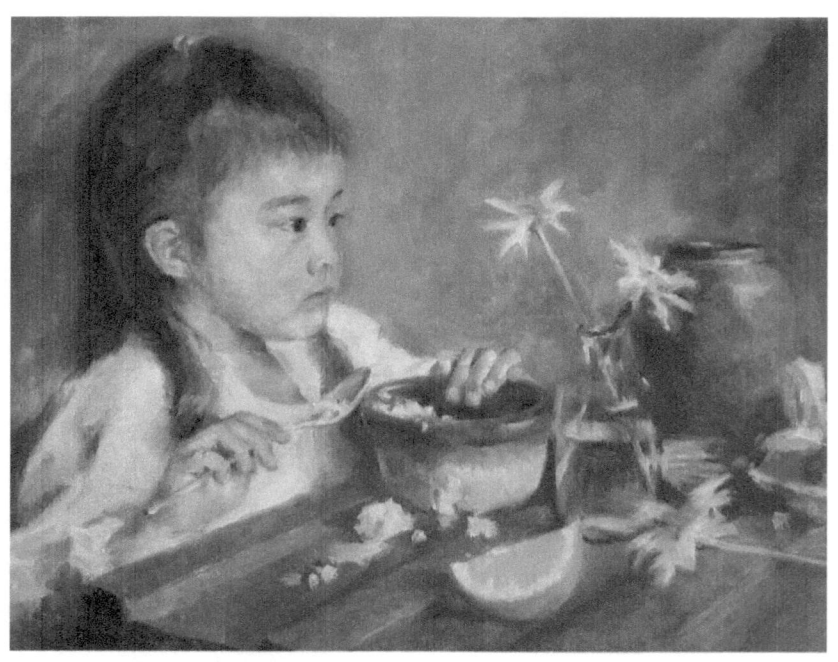

Abby, Oil, by Jaz Xu

Journey of The Soul | Jaz Xu

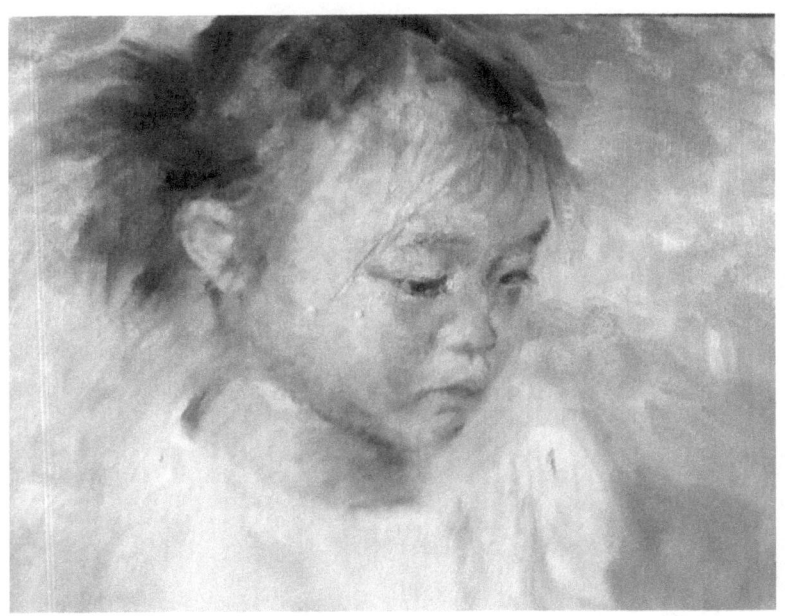

Abby, Oil, by Jaz Xu

Journey of The Soul | Jaz Xu

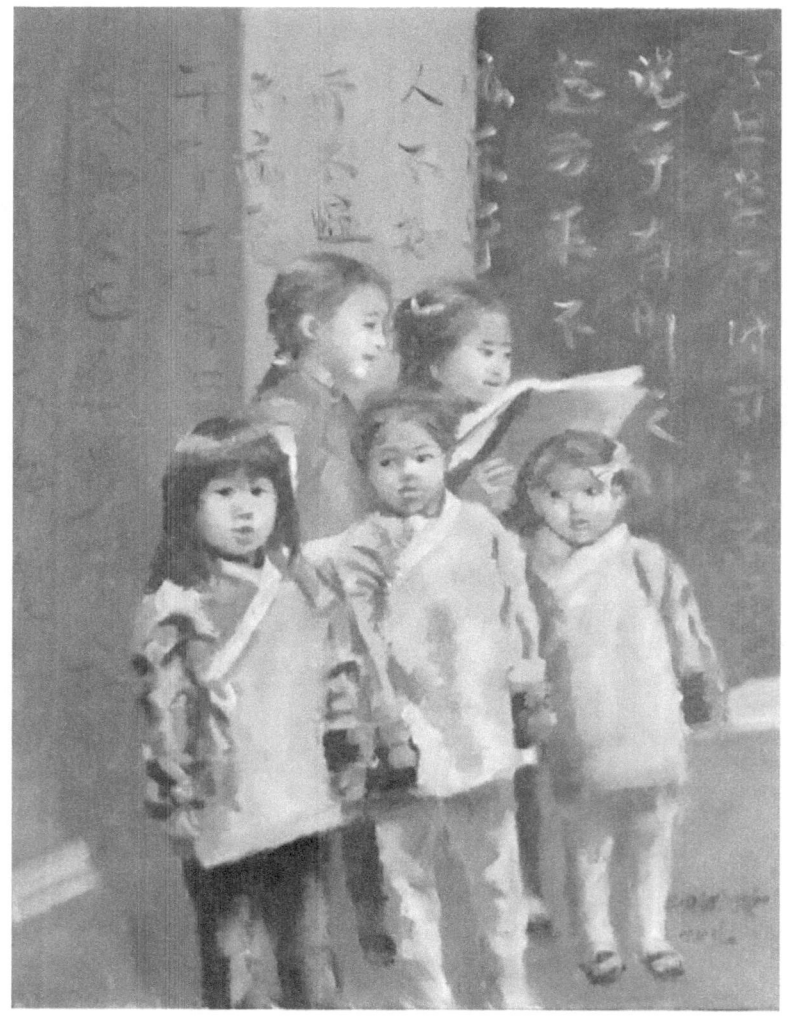

Little Confucius, Oil, by Jaz Xu

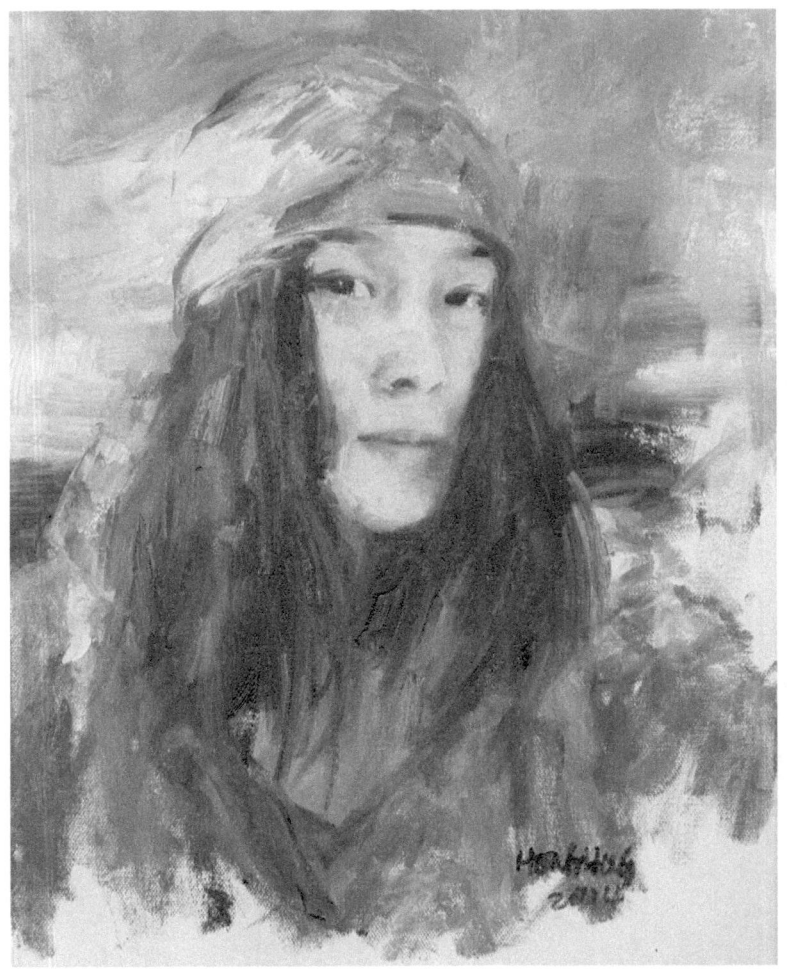

Self Portrait, Oil, by Jaz Xu

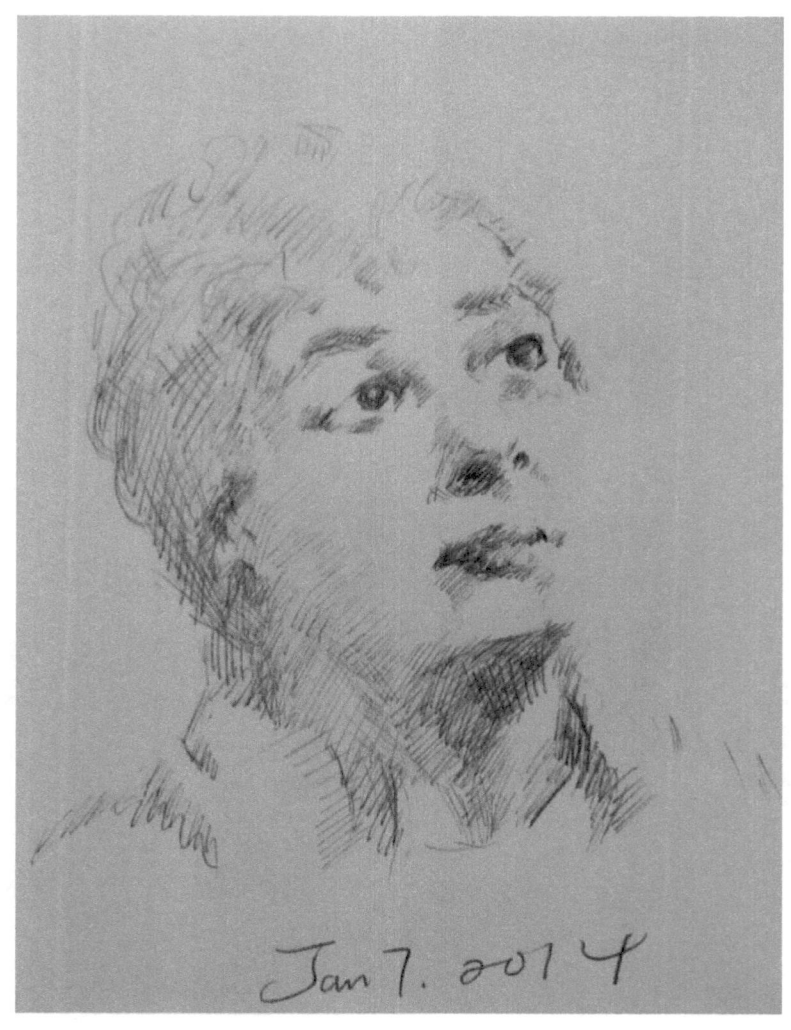

Ink, by Jaz Xu

Journey of The Soul | Jaz Xu

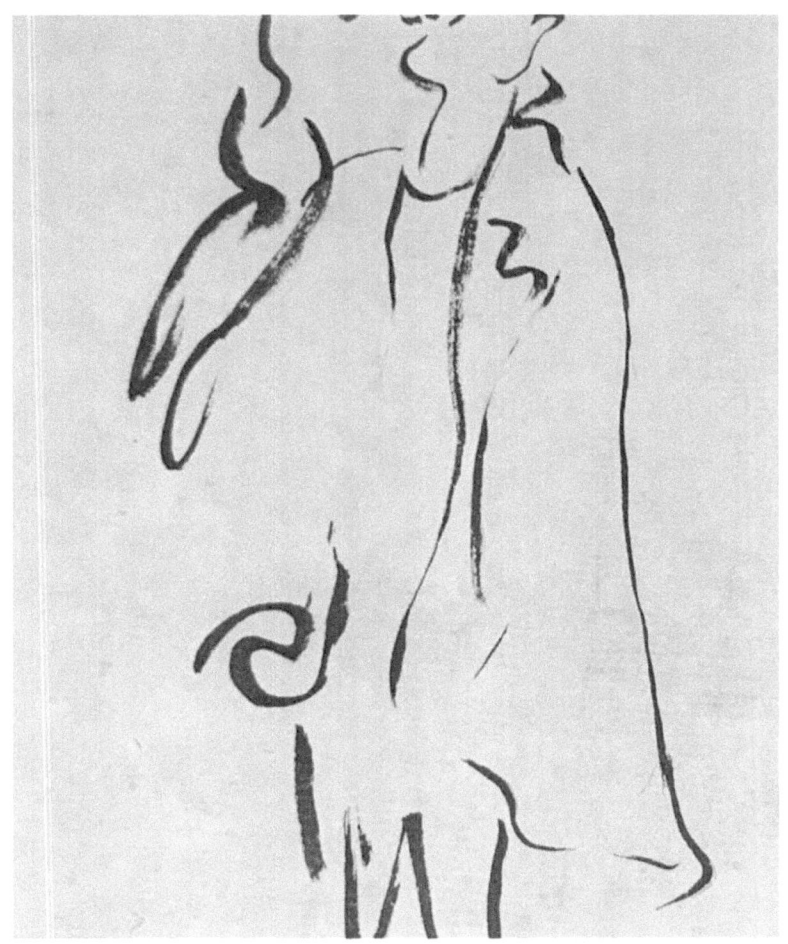

Ink, by Jaz Xu

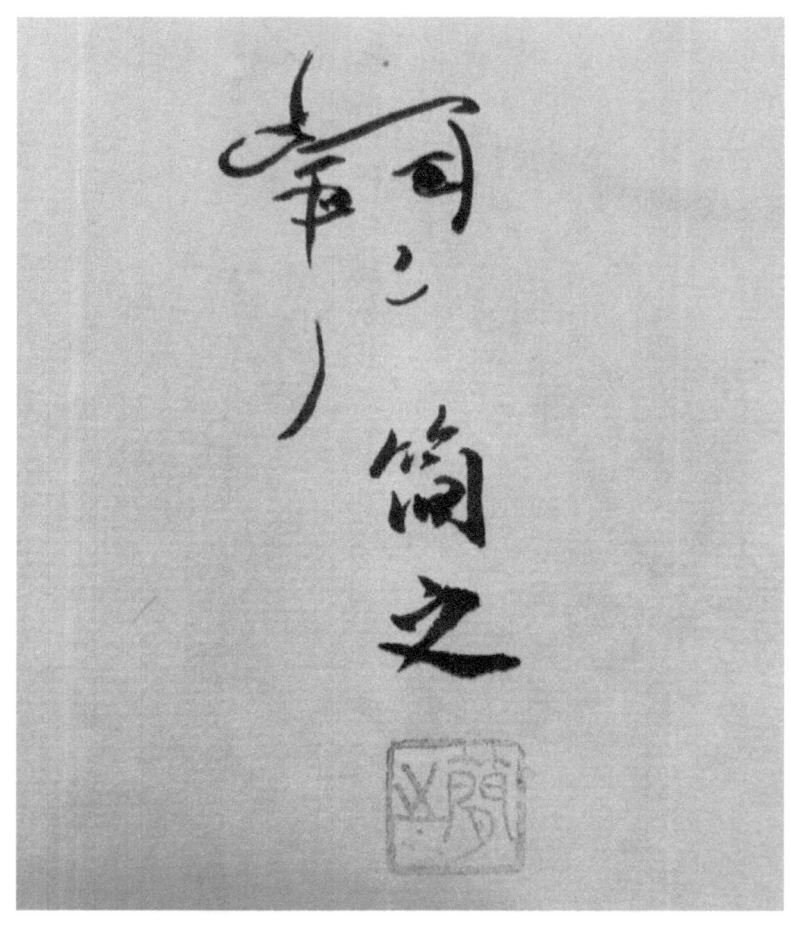

Self Portrait, Oil, by Jaz Xu

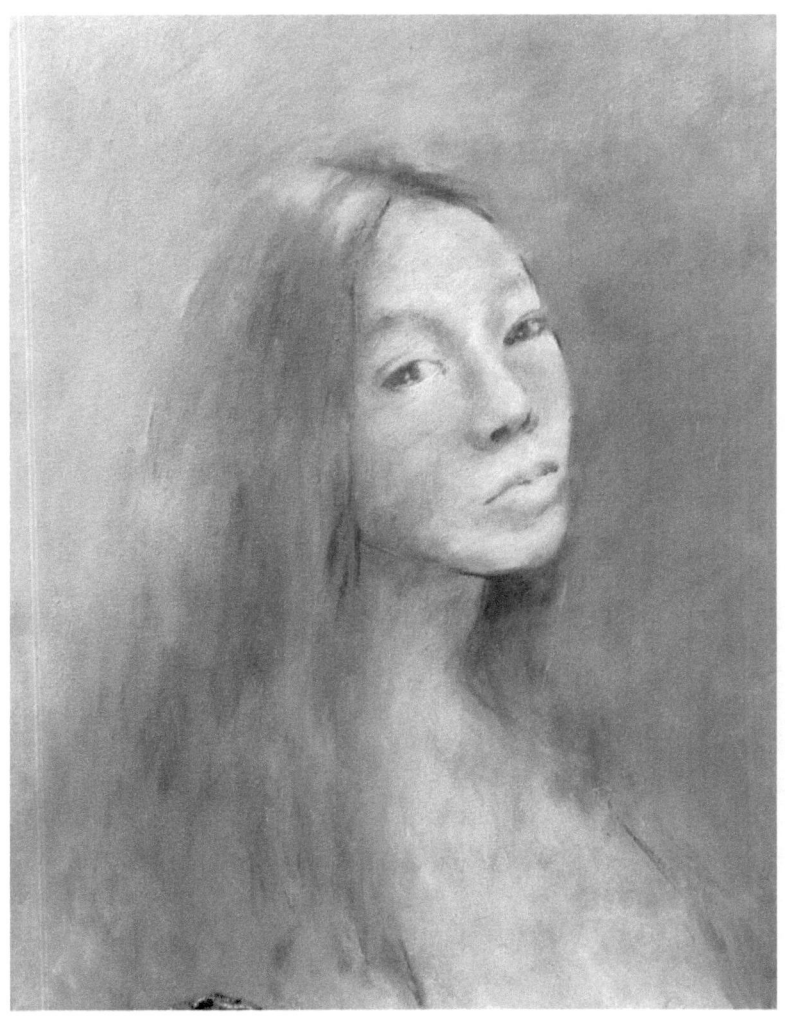

Self Portrait, Oil, by Jaz Xu

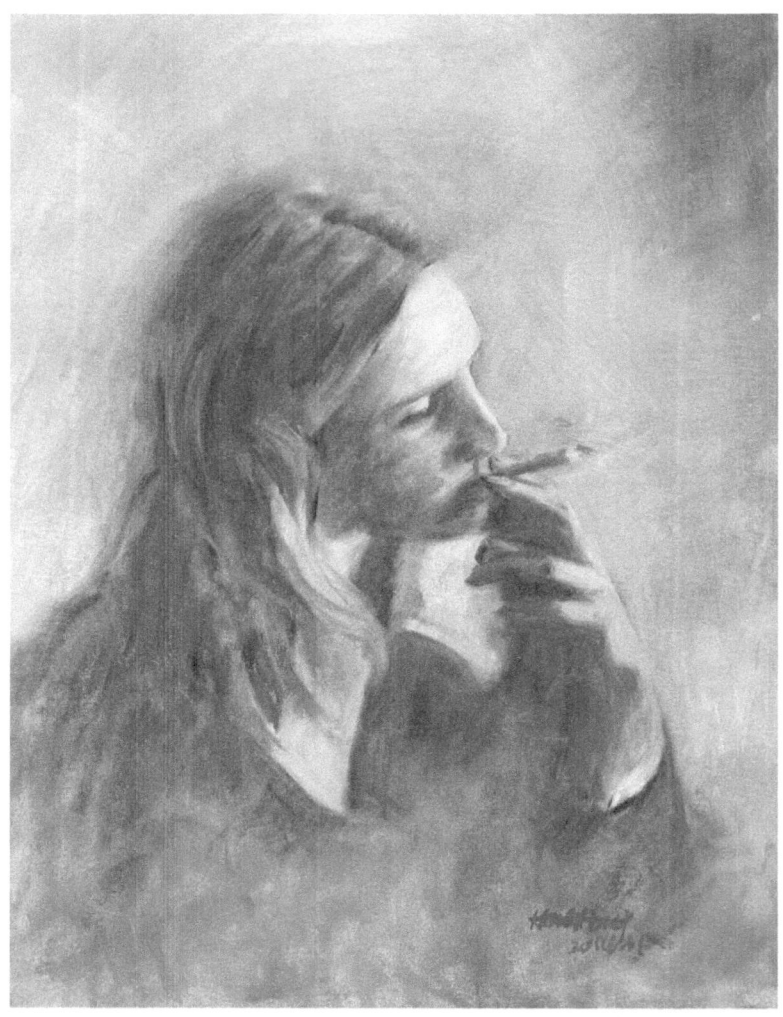

Oil, by Jaz Xu

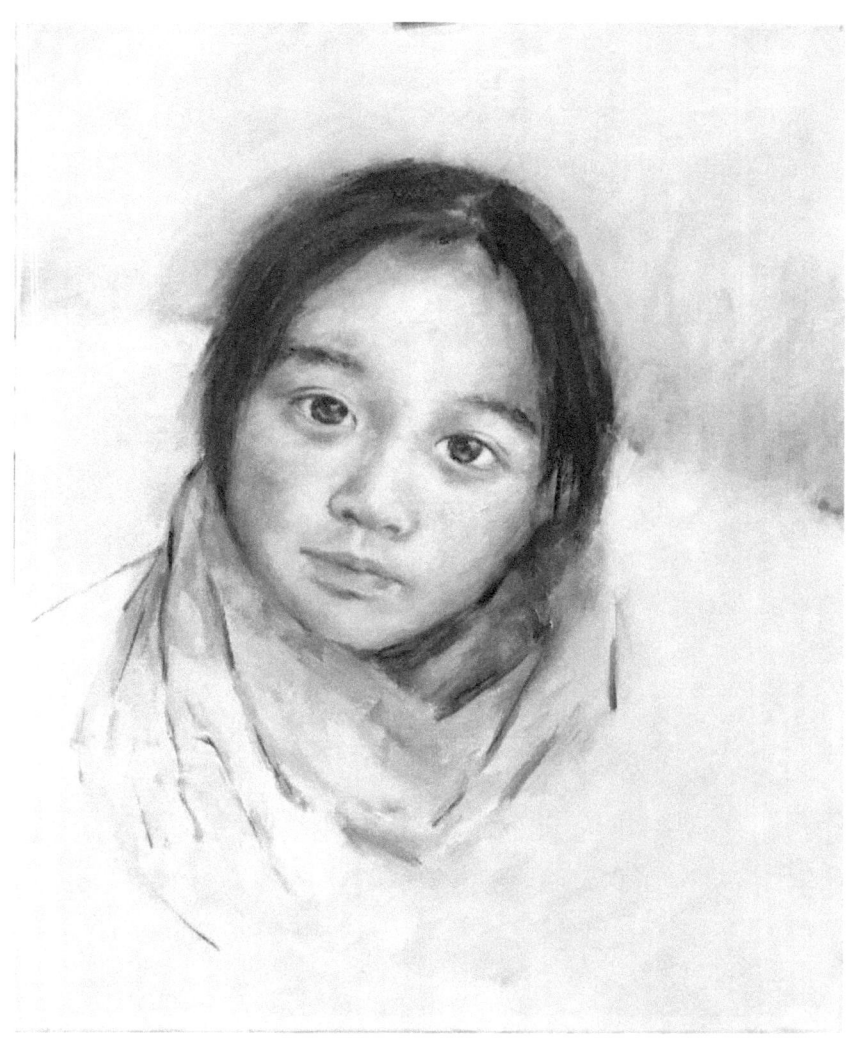

Abby, Oil, by Jaz Xu

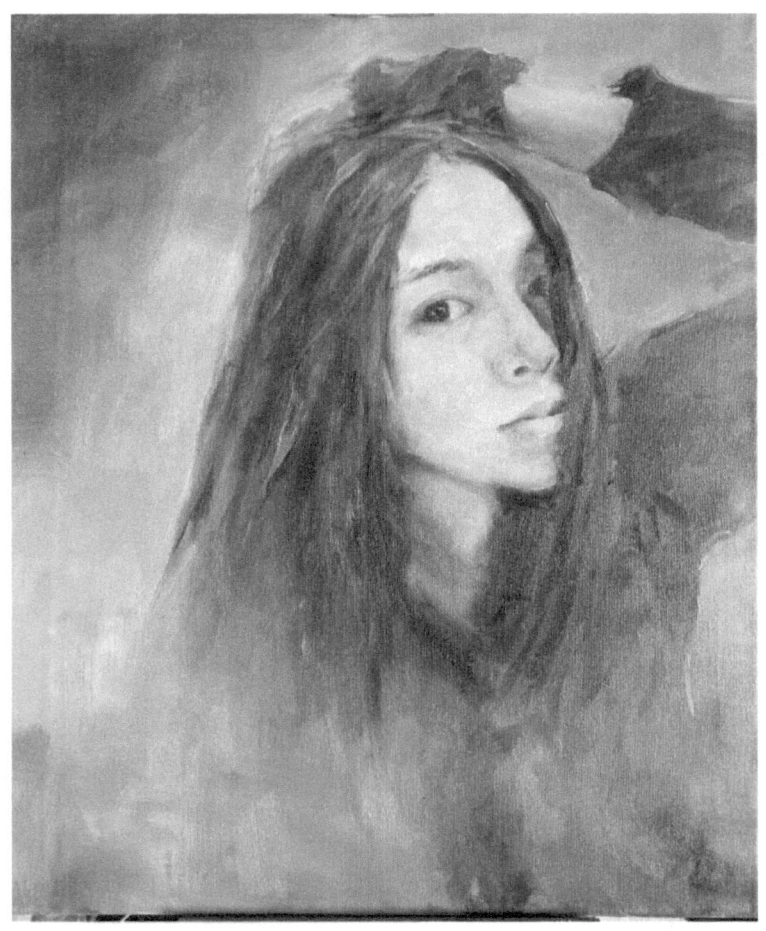

Self Portrait, Oil, by Jaz Xu

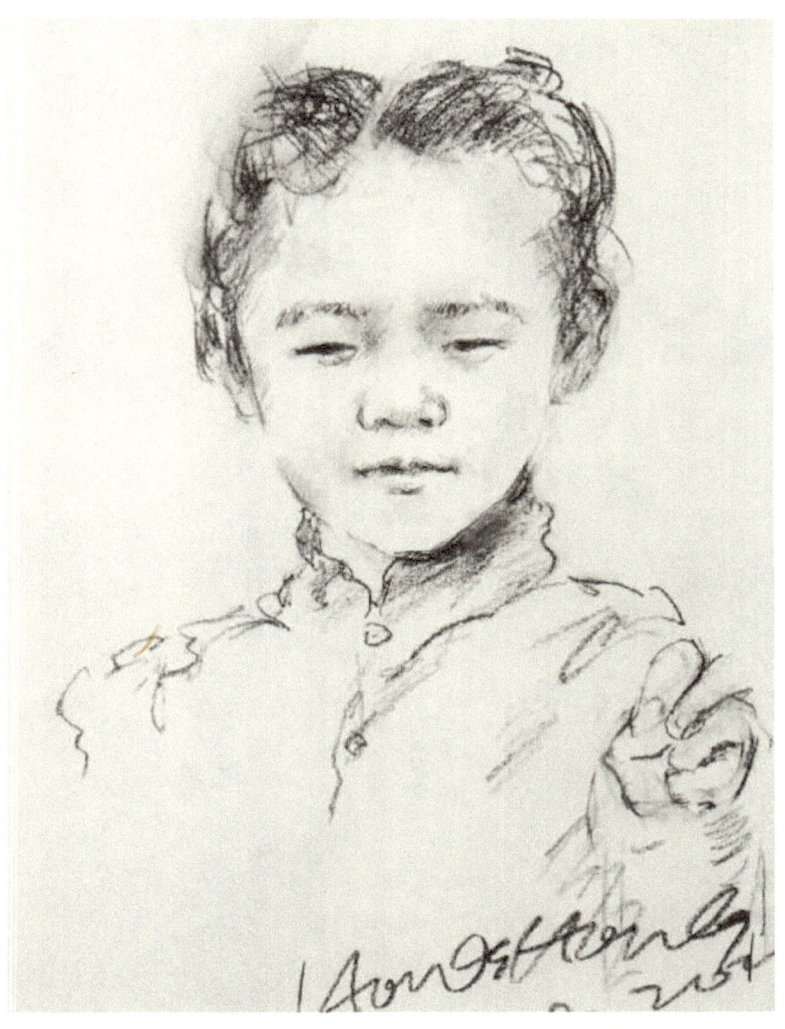

Audrey, Charcoal, by Jaz Xu

Journey of The Soul | Jaz Xu

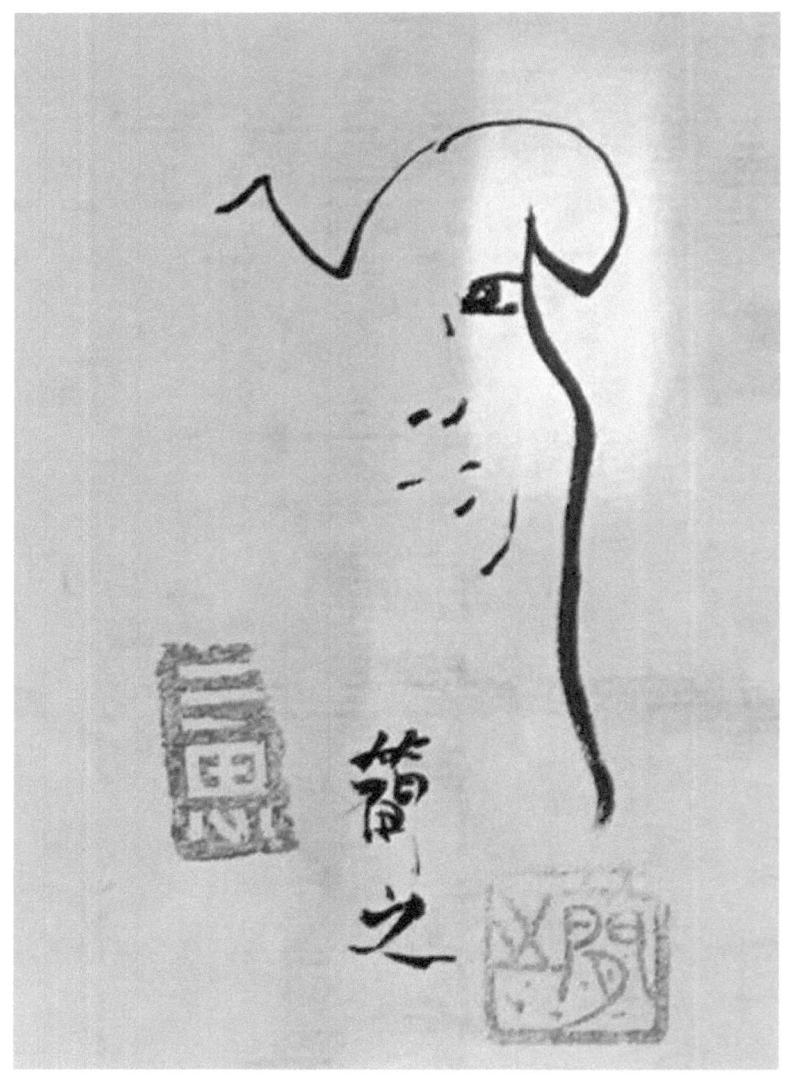

Jaz Xu, Ink

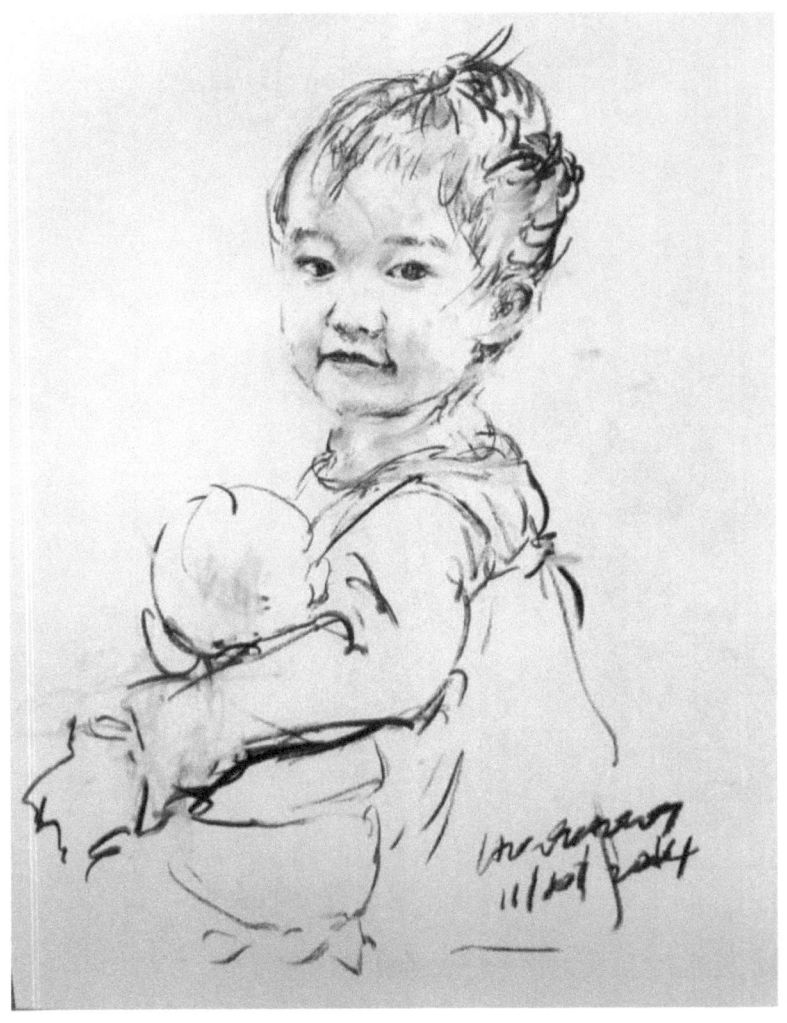

Abby, Charcoal, by Jaz Xu

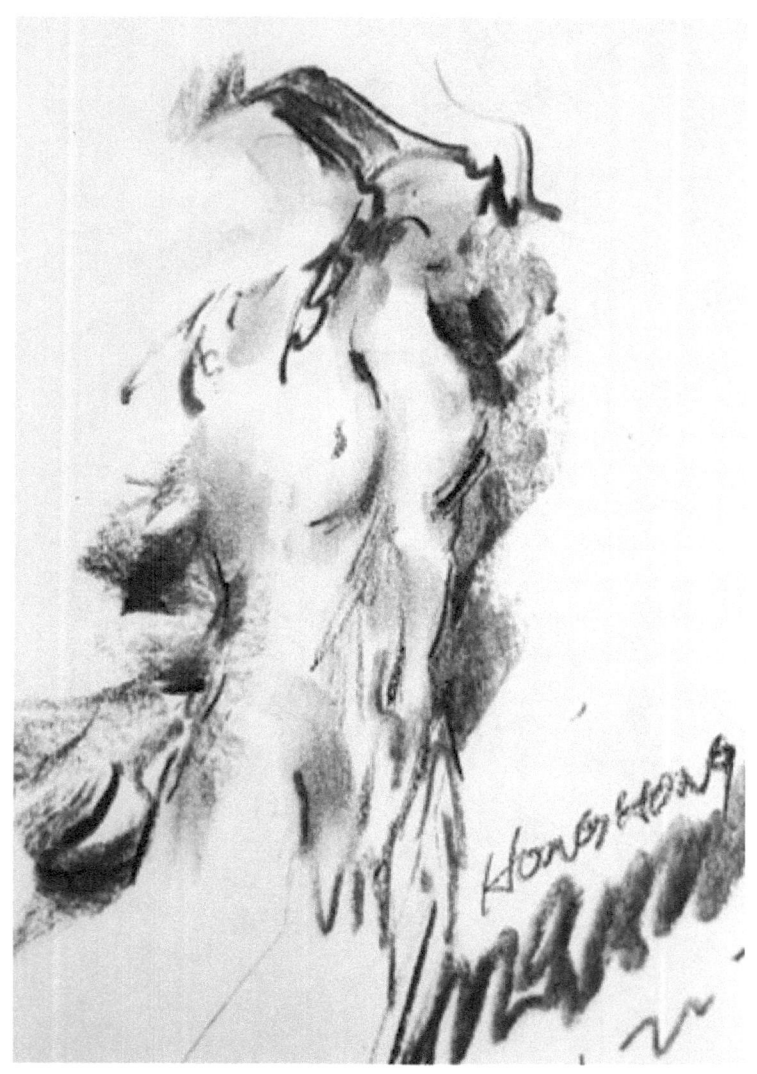

Jaz Xu

About the Author

Jaz Xu is an artist and writer. She loves to paint people and write about their stories as well as her own journey of the soul. She also loves to travel around the world. Jaz lives in her deep inner world, and journeys of her soul emerge through her arts and words to manifest themselves for all to see.

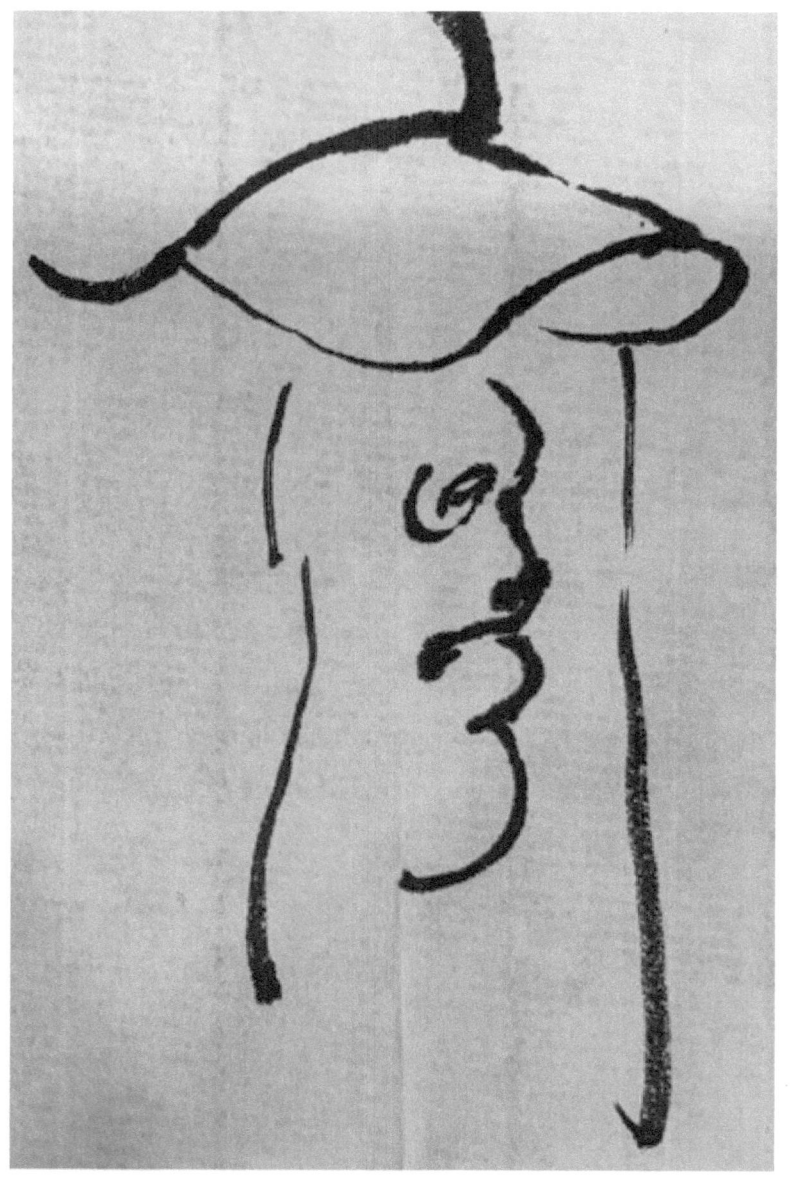

Self Portrait, ink, by Jaz Xu

Journey of The Soul | Jaz Xu

www.ingramcontent.com/pod-product-compliance
Lightning Source LLC
Chambersburg PA
CBHW021434210526
45463CB00002B/515